THE

ART OF

Winning

Government

Grants

THE
ART OF
Winning
Government
Grants

BY HOWARD HILLMAN

Coauthor: Kathryn Natale

THE VANGUARD PRESS, INC.   NEW YORK

*This book is dedicated to
the taxpayer,
without whom
government grants
would be nonexistent*

CONTENTS

Preface

Part One: The Six Grant-Seeking Phases

Introduction to Part One		3
PHASE ONE:	The Preliminaries	5
PHASE TWO:	Researching Your Opportunities	9
PHASE THREE:	Preparing Your Application	22
PHASE FOUR:	Submitting Your Application	43
PHASE FIVE:	The Review of Your Application	46
PHASE SIX:	After the Decision Is Made	52

Part Two: Where The Money Is

Department of Health, Education, and Welfare (HEW)	63
Other U.S. Government Agencies	77
Quasi-Governmental Agencies	100
State and Local Governmental Agencies	110

Part Three: Information Sources

Introduction to Part Three	117
General Tips on Obtaining Information	118
Catalog of Federal Domestic Assistance	124
Federal Register	135
Federal Information Centers	140
Federal Regional Councils	145
Federal Circulars	148
Other Sources of Information	155

Appendixes

A) History and Trends   195
B) Grant Genesis   198
C) The Bureaucratic Monster   201
D) A-95 Clearinghouse Review Process   203
E) Student Aid   208
F) Forms of Address   212
G) Acronyms   215
H) Types of Grants   222
J) Glossary   226

Bibliography   231

Index   235

PREFACE

Over \$100 billion in domestic financial assistance will be doled out this year by the Federal, state, and local governments. Competing for these funds will be millions of individuals, hundreds of thousands of organizations—and, for the federal funds, virtually every state and local government. The purpose of this book is to help you get your fair share, be you a seasoned or neophyte grant-seeker.

Even if your personal political philosophy dislikes the idea of government financial assistance, it is here to stay—and will probably continue to grow. As individuals and organizations in need of operating dollars, we would be doing ourselves a great injustice if we didn't learn how to obtain government funds, because they are paid for out of our tax dollars.

A careful reading of our book will save you needless legwork, journeys into blind alleys, and lost opportunities. For your benefit, we have added to our own prior knowledge of government grants by undertaking an extensive research program. We have interviewed a wide cross section of government grant-seekers in order to pass on to you what they have learned through the costly trial-and-error process. We have spoken with funding-agency officials on all levels, from the file clerk to the top executive. We have met with congressmen and senators, the persons who enact the funding bills. We have read hundreds of books and thousands of articles. Then we have taken all this information and painstakingly boiled it down and organized it for you—the busy, intelligent reader.

While our book can't guarantee you success, it will certainly improve your chances. We wish you a fruitful quest.

PART ONE
The Six Grant-Seeking Phases

INTRODUCTION TO PART ONE

Every grant-seeking endeavor is different. There is no single, all-purpose approach. If there were one, we would give it to you gladly.

What we can give you is a field-tested, time-sequential framework with which to design your customized approach. This formula consists of six basic phases:

Phase 1	The Preliminaries
Phase 2	Researching Your Opportunities
Phase 3	Preparing Your Application
Phase 4	Submitting Your Application
Phase 5	The Review of Your Application
Phase 6	After the Decision Is Made

Each of these six phases will be discussed in detail in separate sections. These distinct phases are not our creation, but a researched historical consensus of what virtually every well-planned government grant-seeking endeavor has gone through.

Even if you have expertise in foundation grant-seeking, you will have to learn and use a new set of tools to win government grants. Though foundation and government grant-seeking pursuits are close cousins, there are some basic critical differences. The government funding agencies, for instance, tend to be more formalized, more accessible in terms of meetings, more willing to negotiate differences, less innovative, and slower to act than their foundation counterparts. Government grant proposals are also generally easier to prepare, the government usually places more administrative controls on the grantee, and the government provides more published information.

Be forewarned. Grant-seeking takes time. Between your initial contact with the government and the receiving of the grant-award decision, plan on six to twelve months, depending on the government agency and program—and on how quickly you prepare and submit the application. Sometimes a two-year period would be a better estimate.

PHASE ONE

The Preliminaries

Before launching your grant-seeking campaign, take time at the onset to make sure that you:

Reverse the roles
Define your goals
Determine your unique sales proposition
Ascertain whether government grants are for you
Develop a plan of action

These factors, as you will see, are interrelated and must be considered more or less concurrently.

Reverse the Roles

If there is one master key to successful government grant-seeking, it is to "reverse the roles." We cannot emphasize this point too strongly.

Reversing the roles means putting yourself in the funding agency's shoes. Rather than thinking (as most grant-seekers do) in terms of how an agency can satisfy your funding needs, determine how you can satisfy the agency's needs. After all, no funding agency gives away money just to give away money—or for specifically helping you as opposed to someone else. Remember, you are not the only deserving beneficiary eligible for the limited funds that are available. Each granting agency dispenses its finite dollars to meet its own well-defined objectives. The closer you fit into its grant-making criteria (without compromising your integrity), the greater the possibility of your being funded.

In short, rather than egocentrically running all over the grant landscape saying, "I have a worthy project—fund me," search out those funding programs that are looking for projects like yours. This creates a natural match-up, which is exactly what you should be seeking.

Define Your Goal

Before you can determine if there is a natural match-up between the agency's goals and yours, you must first define your own project goal. As obvious as this may sound, it is surprising how many otherwise competent grant-seekers bypass this vital step.

An acid test for a sharply defined goal is whether you can state it in a brief paragraph or two. If such a statement requires greater length, your goal is probably still in the hazily defined stage. This will almost certainly impede your grant-seeking endeavor, for unless you know exactly what you want, who will?

To help you define your goal, here are some useful questions to ask yourself about your project. What is the need for the project? What is the project's scope and significance? What are others doing to solve the need? What aspects of the over-all problem can be solved realistically? What is the target population in terms of size, geographical scope, and socioeconomic background? Can the results be measured? Is the project a priority for me, my organization, and my community?

Having answered these questions, try writing a rough draft of your project goal. Writing helps clarify thought. Showing the draft to your colleagues also helps—they can suggest small refinements and are in a position to detect possible blind spots.

Determine Your Unique Sales Proposition

The internationally noted advertising executive David Ogilvy advised his clients to promote the "unique selling proposition" of their product or service. This term refers to what the product or service offers in contrast to what competitive products or services do not offer in the eyes of a particular consumer-population segment.

Government grant-seeking, whether we want to recognize it or not, requires sophisticated marketing skills. Each of your projects is in direct competition with other worthy projects for a limited number of available funding dollars. If you want to be successful, you must compete—and to compete successfully, you must identify and promote what your particular project uniquely offers to the consumer—in this case, the government funding agencies.

To determine your project's "unique selling proposition," you must analyze your project and your organization carefully, poll people outside your organization to ascertain how they view them, learn what the funding agency needs, and make a reasonably thorough analysis of what your grant-seeking competition can and cannot offer to satisfy those needs.

With your "unique selling proposition" clearly defined, you are armed with an invaluable grant-seeking asset: you know your product and territory.

Ascertain whether Government Grants are for You

Too many overzealous fund-seekers jump headlong into the grant-seeking process without first objectively asking themselves, "Should I be seeking government grants in the first place?" Perhaps you are not eligible for the type of government funds you are seeking. Perhaps your personnel and money resources would be more wisely invested in seeking funds from foundations, corporations, service organizations, or even individual contributions. Or perhaps you shouldn't be seeking funds at all. It doesn't matter how fast you're running if you're running up the wrong road.

Even if you find it financially worth your while to seek government funding, you must still ask yourself whether you will be willing to make certain sacrifices that may, for instance, usurp some of your independence. Government grants often come with strings attached. Another potential negative factor to consider is the red tape and bureaucratic headaches that are sometimes inevitable.

These and the other issues that will help you determine whether you should be seeking government grants are discussed throughout this book. After reading it, you will have either the knowledge of how to seek a government grant—or the foresight not to be seeking one. Either way, you'll be ahead of the game.

Develop a Plan of Action

If you are undertaking a limited-scale grant-seeking program, you need not worry about preparing elaborate policies and guidelines. This is especially true if you are an individual. Larger-scale grant-seeking operations, however, should prepare a detailed plan of action if efficiency is to be maximized and internal personnel complex minimized. This master plan should carefully spell out what your organization wants to do and how it will do it (for instance: budget and facilities; required personnel; lines of responsibility and authority).

When outlining your fund-raising objectives, be sure to give serious thought to the semi-distant future. As critical as this advance planning may be, few nonprofit organizations give it the consideration it deserves. They get so wrapped up in their day-to-day crises that they neglect to set aside time to work out a five-year plan on where they're going.

PHASE TWO

Researching Your Opportunities

With the preliminaries out of the way, you are ready to begin working on a time-consuming step: researching your grant opportunities. To make your efforts most effective, you must establish an information-gathering and reference system, and cultivate the necessary contacts.

Establish an Information System

Information is the lifeblood of government grant-seeking. Consequently, establishing a workable information-gathering and reference system is essential, whether you are an individual or a large institutional grant-seeker.

Gathering government-grant information may sound like a simple task, but it isn't, because you run into at least five frustrating obstacles:

There is so much published grant information that you would need a staff of at least a dozen full-time people to read it.

Old information sources become extinct or outdated while new ones are created at a breathtaking pace.

Some of the information—especially that coming directly from the government—is difficult to decipher and comprehend. The U.S. Department of Health, Education, and Welfare (HEW) is so concerned about this situation that it recently required many of its thousand or so rules-writing employees to take special English classes on how to write easily understood regulations.

You'll probably have to deal with a number of different agencies and subunits, since funding responsibilities often overlap. The health field, for instance, has several hundred different programs administered by no fewer than ten major federal departments and independent agencies. Moreover, those programs fall under the jurisdiction of some sixty advisory commissions.

Policies and application procedures vary not only from agency to agency, but also from program to program within agencies. Adding to this complexity are the state and local governmental funding programs, each with its own set of rules.

Despite these obstacles, you really have no choice but to do your very best (based upon your resources) to acquire and digest as much pertinent information as possible. To help you, we have prepared this section and Part III, "Information Sources." Together they will give you the tips, insights, and general background understanding you'll need to get plugged into the government-grant information system—and to start developing an active library tailored to your needs.

When building your library, try to avoid these common weaknesses:

Outdated Information: An obsolete program announcement, guideline, application form, or deadline date can delay or destroy your chances of being funded. Keeping information up to date is costly and boring, but in the long run it is almost always worth the investment.

Insufficient Information: It is as great a sin to have insufficient as it is to have outdated information. With so many programs constantly being altered or begun, you should leave no stone unturned. This means aggressively acquiring information from government publications, agency officials, your congressman, your state and community leaders, your trade organizations and publications, your colleagues and grant-seeking competitors, and nonprofit and commercial information services, to list the major sources.

Noncentralized Information: One person should be responsible for receiving, organizing, maintaining, and disseminating all incoming grant information. He would be your grant-coordinator.

Inaccessible Information: If you should have a grant-coordinator, make sure that this person carries out his responsibilities of insuring that every employee within your organization receives and understands the significance of any grant information that may be relevant to his or her respective position. Regrettably, some grant-coordinators, to enhance their own job security and stature, go so far as to make information seem more esoteric than it really is.

Needlessly Complicated Records: Keep the organization of your reference files and library system as simple as possible. Otherwise you'll be creating potential confusion for new staff members, not to mention wasting time.

Cultivate the Necessary Outside Contacts

When seeking federal grants, six types of outside contacts are especially worth developing:

Funding Program officers
Other Executive Branch officials
Your congressman
Your community leaders
Leadership in your field of interest
Your funding competition

These six types of contacts—each of which will be discussed separately—can play a crucial role in your grant pursuit. Collectively, they provide you with an informal intelligence network of considerable capacity. On more than a few occasions their opinion and/or influence can tip the grant-award decision-making scale in your favor. Despite the undeniable importance of these outside contacts, most grant-seekers seldom, if ever, cultivate them—or if they do, they tend to wait until it is too late. The time to start building outside contacts is now, long before you actually need them. Only then can you be reasonably assured of a reliable access to information before a crisis develops.

Funding Program Officers

The single most valuable type of federal official you can cultivate is usually the officer in charge of the funding program specifically relating to your project.

Depending on the agency, these people—called grant administrators or funding program officers, among other descriptive names—can operate out of national, regional, or local-level offices. They are in an excellent position to provide you with accurate and updated grant information as well as general guidance. Becoming friendly with them is not necessarily an attempt to sway their funding decisions, should they have that power, but rather to establish an authoritative source of information that is but a phone call away. In fact, one of the reasons these public servants are being paid is to keep you abreast of what is happening in their areas of responsibility. Moreover, the Freedom of Information Act (see page 118) more or less requires that they fulfill your information requests.

How does one obtain the name of the appropriate funding program office or officer? There are a number of ways to determine this, including looking under the "Information Contacts" section in the various program listings in the *Catalog of Federal Domestic Assistance.* You can also ask the Federal Information Center nearest you, or the regional office of the appropriate agency.

Having learned the funding program official's name, your next step is to telephone (usually your best bet) or write him or her. Briefly describe your project and ask whether it correlates with the funding program's general objectives. If it does, ask for an exploratory meeting, should one be mutually convenient. If not, develop a written correspondence and telephone-communication relationship with the officer.

If the funding program office is out of town, ask if the official plans to be visiting your city in the near future. (Some funding program officers travel frequently to remain in close contact with their publics.)

Try to set up the meeting as early as possible, because you'll probably need all the lead time you can muster for getting your application in proper form prior to the deadline date.

Ask the official to send you all pertinent literature, including grant procedures and application forms so you can study them prior to the meeting. Also, obtain and read carefully a copy of the enabling legislation (see "Congressional Bills," page 165).

Whoever represents your organization at the meeting should be well informed about your project, its funding competition, and the grant program. He or she should be articulate and capable of making a good impression. If he is well-known, so much the better.

If you are the one attending the meeting, prepare yourself well. Do your homework so thoroughly that you won't have to ask a single question whose answer can be found in readily available literature. You'll probably have only fifteen minutes to an hour—so be brief, concise, and make every minute count.

Be businesslike, but keep the meeting's general tone on a somewhat informal note. The more you treat the officer as a human being, the more he or she will cooperate with you. After all, most government officials love to receive respect, feel appreciated, and help people in need of assistance. They're just like the rest of us.

Don't oversell your project, as this conduct usually raises doubt in the official's mind about its credibility and substance. For the same reason, don't knock your competition.

Try to assess how much decision-making power the official actually has. If the power lies elsewhere, find out who has it. Even if the funding program officer doesn't have the power, remember that he or she usually has indirect influence over the persons who do. Be prepared for the fact that some officials assume power beyond their congressional mandate. A few have been known to award grants counter to the funding intent of Congress. Or sometimes they refuse to release funds that have already been authorized and appropriated. This situation has led a few public-interest groups to sue an agency in court, forcing it to make the required grants.

Avoid using pressure tactics, as this turns off most funding program officers. If, for instance, you have an endorsement from your congressman, use it—but use it delicately.

Write your anticipated questions down in a check-list format —with the most important questions first. Often it pays to give the official a copy. Printed, as opposed to oral, questions usually elicit better answers—especially if the official has to get back to you with the answers at a later date.

Your questions should be phrased as specifically as possible: vague questions invite vague answers or, even worse, a disrespectful reaction on the part of the official. Should the official be vague in his or her answers, don't be shy about repeating or rephrasing your questions. You have a right to be informed.

If the official should say "no" to your project or to any of your probing questions, don't be afraid to ask why—but, at the same time, don't contest his or her judgment unless you have very good reason to do so. Most funding program officers know their subject sufficiently well to ascertain whether your project meets their program's criteria—or whether you have to alter part of your project to be eligible for the funds.

When an alteration is suggested, try to be flexible. As we emphasized in the opening of this book, you should reverse roles and satisfy the agency's goal (so long as you don't violate the integrity of your own project).

Guard against becoming falsely hopeful or pessimistic because of misconstruing what a program officer tells you. Listen carefully for nuances. Ask for clarification any time you aren't sure of the exact nature and meaning of the information being given you. For instance: Are the funds being discussed actually appropriated or merely authorized? And be sure to take accurate notes. This procedure will protect you against memory loss as well as flatter the official.

The specific questions to be asked will, of course, vary from project to project, grant-seeker to grant-seeker. To help you start preparing your list, we have compiled this check list of some of the questions experienced grant-seekers have asked funding program officers:

Exactly what type of projects are you—the funding agency—looking for?

What are the chances of my project being funded?

Who is my chief competition?

How much money will be awarded to individual projects similar to mine?

How much of the total appropriation is still available in my project category?

Is there any chance that the funds may be withheld, subject to presidential recission, et cetera?

Exactly what cost categories (direct and indirect) does your program support and not support? What categories do you consider borderline cases?

Am I or my organization subject to restrictions or special requirements?

To whom should the proposal be submitted?

What are the deadline dates?

Is this program subject to the A-95 Review Process (see Appendix D) or any other governmental procedure?

By whom is the funding decision made? What do they look for? What displeases them? What have been their past grant-making patterns?

Would you or someone else in your organization be willing to visit our facilities?

Will your agency be holding special instructional meetings for grant-seekers?

How can I alter my project so it better qualifies for your funding program?

How can my written application be strengthened in terms of content? Format? Length? Style? Third-party endorsements?

Will you look over and make constructive suggestions on my final application before I officially submit it?

Do you know of other current, pending, or future funding programs that offer me good funding opportunities?

Can you put me and/or my organization on your permanent mailing list for program announcements, newsletters, et cetera?

When the official asks you a question, be honest and straightforward. If you don't know the answer, freely admit your ignorance. To do otherwise may jeopardize not only this funding opportunity, but many future ones.

More often than not, subsequent contact with the funding program officer is needed to clear up vague or unsettled questions and issues—and to obtain advice on preparing and submitting your proposal. This dialogue can be in the form of a letter, telephone call, or a meeting. In the last instance, you can get together at the officer's place, your office (called a site or on-site visit) or, perhaps, over lunch.

One word of warning about entertaining U.S. Government officials. Some are statutorily forbidden to accept gratuities such as a free lunch—so discretely inquire about this matter ahead of time. Even if the no-lunch restriction exists, there is nothing to stop the two of you from going Dutch.

On-site visits are desirable and sometimes mandatory. They are desirable from your point of view because they give the funding agency officer an opportunity to meet your personnel and to observe your operation and facilities firsthand. This personalizes your organization in the agency's mind, thereby probably strengthening your grant-winning chances. On-site visits are mandatory for certain types of grants, especially for those involving technical competence or large sums of money. They are required or strongly suggested if the grant-applicant is relatively unknown or has not previously dealt with the agency. On-site visits can last anywhere from an hour to a day, seldom longer.

Other Executive Branch Officials

Besides the funding program officer, there are a number of other Executive Branch officials worth cultivating. Of special potential value are key staff members of the regional offices of the big agencies. They can usually provide you with decentralized information not normally disseminated by their national headquarters. And sometimes the personnel in these regional offices have the decision-making power to award grants.

But don't overlook headquarters personnel, especially if the nature and scale of your project is grand—if you live in or near, or make frequent visits to Washington, D.C., if you are particularly adept at building and maintaining a relationship by means of correspondence or the telephone, and/or if one of your former colleagues now works for the agency. (The shuttling of executives back and forth between the government and private sector is a common Washington phenomenon.)

The hierarchical structures of government agencies vary, but the following schematic diagram will give you a general idea of the classic pyramidal chain of command typical of most of the large, cabinet-level departments:

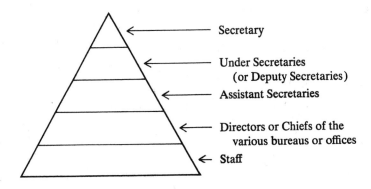

Your contacts need not be highly placed as long as they are well placed. Strange as it may seem to someone not familiar with the workings of the U.S. Government, a middle-ranked official holding the right job can usually do more for you than if your old school roommate, the President of the United States, recommends that your project be funded. In the business world, a company president usually has the power to make anyone in the organization comply with his or her wishes, but in the world of the government, elected officials have to contend with a great deal of independence. This semiautonomy is mainly fostered by the civil service system and the unmanageable size of the Federal government.

You may not always know the right contact level to cultivate. When in doubt, it is almost always better to have too high rather than too low a power on your side.

A broad-based variety of contacts is also helpful as funding programs for your particular project may now or in the future come from a number of sources, not just the obvious ones. The more widely dispersed your contacts, the quicker you'll be able to learn about and react to new and revised programs—long before the information appears in official government sources such as the *Federal Register* and the *Catalog of Federal Domestic Assistance*.

Whenever possible, write to an official by name, not just by title. This shows the official you are at least somewhat familiar with his or her bailiwick. It is also flattering. Unearthing the official's name, however, can be difficult because of the complexity of the government and the normal job turnover. There are a number of publications containing personnel directories, including the *Congressional Directory, Congressional Staff Directory, Directory of Key Government Personnel, U.S. Government Manual,* and *Washington Information Directory*. All are described in Part III, "Information Sources." In addition, each agency has its own specialized personnel directory, which can be obtained free or for a small charge, depending on the agency's policy. Other sources are your nearest Federal Information Center and the switchboard or information center of the appropriate agency.

Always bear in mind that the quality of information sources varies because not all government employees are as well informed or as cooperative as one might expect them to be. For instance, one seeker of grant information telephoned HEW to find the name of its secretary, the chief executive. The HEW employee gave the inquirer the name of the former HEW secretary, who had left the position well over a year before.

Your Congressman

While your senator usually has considerably more political clout, your congressman will probably be more willing to take the time to help you. Assistance can come in two forms: political influence and information.

"Political influence": does a congressman have this power over an Executive Branch funding agency? While many agency spokesmen deny the existence of this influence, it seems naive to do so. Influence will exist as long as Congress continues to vote on each agency's budget (though the magnitude of this influence is no longer what it used to be during the old days of back-room government).

When you obtain the benefits of congressman's influence, however, don't overestimate its effectiveness. For instance, you may be able to get your congressman to write a letter of endorsement to the funding agency officer. This official may merely give lip service to the congressman's letter by replying "Thank you for your letter. I will certainly give the project my fullest consideration," or similar words, thereby seeming to take a personal interest but in fact nothing special.

Each congressman's political power depends on a number of factors. Perhaps the most important ones are your representative's position and tenure in Congress. A member of the Appropriations Committee, for example, is in a position to exert considerable influence. Also, if, for example, your project involves agriculture and your congressman or a congressman you know sits on the agricultural subcommittee, the endorsement for your project will increase in value.

On balance, while the degree of effectiveness of a congressman's political influence has and will continue to be debated, some influence does exist—and it would be foolish not to secure that influence for yourself, no matter how slight it may be. Otherwise you may lose an invaluable competitive edge, because at least a few of your funding competitors will be securing congressional influence for themselves.

While the value of congressional assistance in the form of political influence is moot, there is no doubt that such assistance in the form of information is significant and worthwhile. If you're having difficulty in getting a direct answer from an agency official, low-keyed prodding by your congressman may help. Your representative's letter or telephone call to an agency can also help speed up the normally slow process of getting published material.

Your representative's office is also an excellent source of congressionally generated information. The staff can put you on the mailing list for congressional newsletters and other publications on subjects relating to your project.

When cultivating your congressman, make sure you cultivate his or her staff as well, including the two top-ranking employees, the administrative and legislative assistants.

Your Community Leaders

The support of your community leaders is becoming increasingly important because federal funding agencies, more now than in the past, are looking for proof that a project has local-level backing. If you are seeking state or local funds, community-leadership contacts will play an even more vital role.

Leaders in Your Field of Interest

What you can learn from the leaders in your field of interest is significant, as the very nature of their roles usually keeps them knowledgeably informed on forthcoming government programs. These leaders can also be of invaluable service to you in the endorsement capacity, as the Federal government is seeking more evidence that projects have intradisciplinary support.

Your Funding Competition

Many grant-seekers shy away from sharing information with their funding competitors for fear of being nosed out by them for a grant. History has shown that the majority of the truly successful grant-seekers realize they can't learn everything by themselves, so they frequently get together with their counterparts in other grant-seeking organizations to share information. A rewarding synergistic exchange results.

PHASE THREE

Preparing Your Application

Picture an individual (or committee) sitting at a desk trying to decide whether your grant application should be funded. In front of this person is your application and its attendant material. These pieces of paper are practically all the evaluator has on which to base his or her decision. Nowhere is there a "you" who can personally look over the decision-maker's shoulder to clear up any questions that may arise concerning your grant quest. Obviously, knowing the ins and outs of preparing a well-written application is critical.

Many grant-seekers who have had splendid projects have lost out on grants because they made errors in the preparation of their application. Our research has shown that certain errors occur over and over again. The ten most common ones (not ranked in any special order) are individually discussed in this section.

Common Error #1: Wrong Application Forms/Instructions

It would certainly be convenient if the Federal government had one standardized grant-application form, but it doesn't—and probably never will, despite the fact that it is currently experimenting with one. Each agency (and even some agency subunits) loves creating its own form either because unique programs require them or because of each agency's stubborn desire to do things its own way. Moreover, some agencies constantly revise their application forms and instructions. To add further confusion, some agency programs—such as the National Science Foundation's Grants for Scientific Research—don't even have printed forms.

All of this increases the grant-seeker's chances of using incorrect or out-of-date application forms and instructions. Such action regrettably causes delay or denial of grants to otherwise qualified grant-seekers. The situation can be easily avoided by a verifying phone call to the appropriate funding program officer.

Common Error #2: Not Following Instructions

As boring as they may be, carefully read—and reread—the instructions that accompany the application. Otherwise you may lose valuable time (or the grant itself) when the agency returns or rejects the improperly completed form.

You will sometimes come across an item on an application form that is too limiting or inflexible to suit your purposes. In such a case, you may have to squeeze a vital piece of information into some other portion of the application form.

If you are unsure of an instruction or of how much license you can take in altering its intent, write or call the funding program officer for clarification rather than take an unnecessary chance.

Common Error #3: Procrastination

Being human, most grant-application preparers dilly and dally, seemingly unable to get started until the deadline date is imminent. Procrastination is a serious error because you need all the lead time you can find—for two major reasons. First, you must have sufficient time to develop and refine your application draft. Second, as will be explained in "Phase 4: Submitting Your Application," you should send in your application comfortably ahead of the funding agency's deadline date.

The most difficult part of preparing an application is taking the first step. After that, momentum grows—especially if you've done your preliminary research and have the proper forms and instructions. Your application practically writes itself.

Start with a first draft. Don't worry at this point about grammar or spelling. You'll have plenty of time to correct such errors later. Also, don't be concerned about missing facts and/or details. One of the purposes of preparing the first draft is to help you determine which items, if any, are still missing, undocumented, or nebulous.

Common Error #4: Poor Writing

Most of the space on the majority of application forms is devoted to fill-in boxes. These blank spaces ask for short answers, demanding only that the preparer have the necessary facts, not language skill. For instance "Name of Official:_____."

All well and good. But most applications also require some type of narrative description of the proposed project. This necessitates a fair command of English, at least in 99 percent of the cases.

Yes, the 1 percent exception does exist, as the following description of a grant verifies:

The purpose of this project is to develop the capability for institutions of higher learning and community agencies and organizations to coalesce for the development of community services and create a model for the coordination of such services that would maximize the available resources from a number of institutions and provide communication and priority needs and response of the educational needs of a given community.

Believe it or not, this description was written by—of all organizations—the Illinois Board of Higher Education. It's possible that you can write a similarly sounding proposal and win—but don't count on it.

In the hope of increasing your winning chances, we present

the following writing tips that are particularly applicable to preparing grant applications:

As you write, try to visualize the reader. Remember, your words will be read by a human being, not by an abstract government entity.

Write in a warm style (the reader's heart is seldom touched by impersonal writing). At the same time, respect the reader's time by being brief and to the point.

When describing your project, emphasize the human element (how people will benefit) rather than abstract ideas and inanimate objects (such as equipment and buildings).

Write objectively. A seasoned evaluator can see through (and is often turned off by) rhetoric.

Convey clear, specific thoughts. Hazy thinking is easily detected by an experienced evaluator.

Back up your assertions with concrete examples and facts. Sweeping generalizations do more harm than good.

Exciting language stimulates and sustains reader interest. For instance, use image-creating adjectives ("the lonely senior citizen") if they accurately describe conditions. Also use the active voice ("We will help drug addicts") rather than the passive voice ("Drug addicts will be helped by us").

Avoid pompous words like "utilize" when "use" has exactly the same meaning.

Try to be aware of possible innuendos. One misused word can alter the evaluator's concept of your project.

Stay clear of professional jargon, because someone reading your proposal may be offended by or may not be familiar with the trade lingo. If you must use a technical or uncommon word, define it in layman terms (remember, while the evaluator is probably an expert in your field, other readers at the agency may not be as knowledgeable).

Use simple sentence structure. Awkward or complex sentence structure slows down the reader and may hinder understanding.

Write in a positive, confident tone without seeming boastful.
Be truthful about your limitations—but discuss them non-
   apologetically.
Finally, write, edit, and rewrite the narrative portion of your
   application—again and again.

Common Error #5: Poor Project Description

The narrative portion of the application usually asks you to
describe your project. This can be an opportunity or a stumbling
block, depending on whether or not you know how to write a
project description. In the event that you don't, we'll take a few
moments to summarize the basics:
A program description should flow in smooth, logical order.
The first three basic sequential steps are:

NEED
↓
OBJECTIVE
↓
METHODS

In most cases, the "need" has already been delineated for
you in general terms by the funding agency. Essentially, this
need is the situation the funding program hopes to alleviate or
eliminate. For instance, a day-care-center grant program is
created because—in the eyes of the agency—certain people need
such services. Your task is to link your project to the need
recognized by the funding agency. In doing so you must establish the fact that the need exists within your administrative
bailiwick, geographic area, or whatever.
In substantiating this need, you must tell who your target
beneficiaries are in terms of number, geographic scope, and
socioeconomic status. You must also quantify the degree of the
need—and establish that no one else is going to satisfy it. It is a
serious mistake to assume the agency shares your assessment,

so supply documented evidence such as hard statistics and impartial expert opinions.

The next two steps, the "objective" and the "methods," are often confused by proposal writers. Your "objective" is what you desire to accomplish, while your "methods" are what you plan to do to achieve your objective. In other words, your "methods" are the means to the end, while your "objective" is the end itself.

It would be incorrect, therefore, to state in a proposal "Our objective is to establish a day-care center," since this is a method. The objective is "To help mothers get back into the work force."

A good objective must meet three criteria: First, it must be attainable. This requires, among other factors, that you have the needed time, resources, expertise, and outside cooperation. Second, your objective must be practical. Building a day-care center for a billion dollars is certainly attainable, but wouldn't be cost-effective. Third, your objective must be measurable in quantitative terms. In the case of a day-care center, perhaps you could calculate the decrease in welfare payments to the new working mothers.

Your objective should coincide as closely as possible with the agency's program objective. If the agency program wants to help left-handed retired seamen find gainful part-time employment in small New England fishing villages, that's the objective you should have. It would be foolish to think you can change the agency's goal. It would be even more foolish to misrepresent your objective—or to alter it to the point where your project loses its self-integrity—just to qualify for the grant. Either way, you'd probably pay for your truth-stretching sooner or later.

To achieve your objective, you have at your disposal a variety of methods—some better than others. It is your responsibility to make sure you've chosen the best methods. You must also convince the grant-application evaluator of this fact (see the "Insufficient Documentation" section below).

The length of your program description will be determined by a variety of factors, including the agency's wishes (ask the funding program officer) and the degree of technical difficulty of your project. When in doubt about the length, brevity is the best rule. But don't be so succinct that you leave out an essential thought or step. The grant world is filled with instances where omissions have spelled the difference between an applicant receiving grant dollars or a refusal. These unsuccessful grant-seekers mistakenly assumed that the evaluator was more aware of their grasp of the problem than was actually the case.

Common Error #6: Insufficient Documentation

It is reckless to think the grant-application evaluator will accept your assessment of the need, the applicability of your objective, and the quality of your methods. The same is true in regard to qualifications of your organization and its personnel. You must anticipate the evaluator's queries and succinctly answer them within the application itself. For a list of some of these potential queries, see page 48.

Sometimes you have so much essential documentation that it is impossible to include all of it in the application itself. Your best bet then is to put the most significant supporting data in the body of the application and put the remaining data in an addendum, if that is allowed by the funding agency program. This back-up material should be selective and neatly packaged. It could include certifications, endorsement letters, vitae of your key personnel, supporting statistics and charts, newspaper clippings and visual material depicting your activities, a summation of your other funding sources, a survey report on what's happening within your discipline, and an annual report. The last item can be a simple one-page affair or a more elaborate publication, depending upon your budget and organization size. A primer worth studying is the 71-page *Creative Annual Reports* pamphlet. For a copy, mail $2.50 to

National Public Relations Council of Health and Welfare
  Services,
419 Park Avenue,
New York, New York 10016.

Common Error #7: Legal Blind Spots

If you submit a grant application and it is accepted, it usually
becomes a binding legal contract. In essence, you have com-
mitted yourself and/or your organization to perform specific
work. Some grant-seekers forget this point and get into trouble
when they don't have the needed time, manpower, facilities, and
other resources to perform the job satisfactorily. Another legal
blind spot involves copyrights, patents, trade secrets, and
purchased equipment. The applicant forgets to establish who
will have the right to these properties upon completion of the
project. Consequently, when preparing your application, you or
your lawyer should check out those small fine points that can
later become huge headaches.

Common Error #8. Money Sent to Wrong Person

When applying for federal funds, you usually designate who
should receive the government check. This person or office can
be your president, executive director, treasurer, finance office,
comptroller, or you, among other possibilities (providing that
the check recipient meets the agency's criteria). A predicament
you want to avoid is having the money pass through the hands
of a bureaucratic type within your organization who can delay
the flow of your hard-won funds in order to increase his or her
power. It happens too often. You also don't want your funds
administered by a person or office that may innocently bottle-
neck your money because of a heavy work load, vacation
schedule, illness, or job turnover.

Common Error #9: No Outside Feedback

When writing your application, try to work closely with the funding program officer. He or she is usually willing to look over your application draft and give constructive criticism. Also, give copies of your application draft to your colleagues and to outside experts for them to review, especially if your proposed project is technical in nature.

Common Error #10: Poorly Conceived Budget

Last but not least among the common errors is preparing an ill-conceived budget.

Think of a budget as a translation of your project into dollars and cents. It must be accurate and well presented if the funding agency is to measure the effectiveness of your project. If your budget falls short of these qualities, the funding agency will be highly reluctant to fund your project.

The required or suggested format will vary from agency to agency and often from program to program. Some agencies and programs have standardized forms, so firmly structured that you need only fill in the numbers. This can be a blessing—or a handicap if your project has unique traits defying simple categorization. If your project's budget can't comfortably fit into the rigid fill-in-the-blank format, you may have to bend the instructions a little (but first get a tacit approval from the funding program officer). Other agencies and programs leave the choice of budget format more or less to you.

Should budget preparation not be your calling, find a qualified individual to help you. Remember, your application will probably be scrutinized by trained accountants when it is evaluated at the agency.

Enlisting an experienced accountant to assist you is not enough, however. You and this person must familiarize yourselves thoroughly with the general and specific budget rules and guidelines dictated by the agency. You must also check and double-check other inputs, including your organization's accounting and payroll personnel, your vendors, the persons who will be performing the project, and the funding program officer. Leave no information stone unturned.

The degree of financial detail you include within your budget will depend largely upon three variables: the wishes of the funding agency and the complexity and nature of your project. Expenses for an innovative program, for instance, will probably have to be explained and justified in more detail than would be the case for a standardized program that has been in existence for a number of years. Except in special circumstances, plan to devote no more than one or two pages of single-spaced copy to your budget.

How much should you ask for? Your wisest course is to be as realistic as possible—requesting too little money can be just as detrimental as padding your budget. You'll always find a grant-seeker or two who argue that you should fatten your budget to leave room for negotiation, because the agency's going to pare your figures anyway. This is not true, at least in more than 95 percent of the cases. If an agency is going to cut your budget, it will probably be for other than an "automatic" reason. Under some circumstances, an agency may even suggest you raise it, as could be the case if the agency wants you to perform an extra service. Perhaps most important of all, federal agency officials have learned, through experience, to smell padded budgets around the corner—and when they do, you can be assured that your application's chances will gravely suffer.

At the same time, don't do yourself harm by underestimating or overlooking some budget item, as neophyte grant-seekers are wont to do. An upshot of these oversights may be that the agency will think you really don't have a sufficient understanding of what must be done to perform your project successfully. Even worse, should your application be accepted, you and/or your organization may have to pay for the underestimated item out of your own pocket, thereby changing your project from an opportunity into a financial yoke.

Still another potential pitfall is not accurately estimating the length of time needed to complete your project. When you take into account the salary factor, this type of error can become particularly costly because it will probably be you—not the government—who will be shelling out the extra payroll checks.

Watch out also for typographic and arithmetic errors. Such mistakes occur more frequently than you might imagine. If the evaluator spots the error, your application may be returned to you, thereby causing a delay or a missed deadline. If the evaluator doesn't spot the error, he or she may come up with a gross misconception about the nature of your proposal and its required budget.

The normal budgetary period for a government grant is one year or less. Even if your grant period is for more than a year, the agency can financially commit itself only to a twelve-month duration at most. Beyond that period renewal is subject to the will of Congress. In the event that you are preparing a budget stretching into future years, your budget for year 2 and thereafter need not be as detailed as for year 1. When estimating these multi-year budgets, don't forget to take into consideration factors such as inflation and merit wage increases.

When preparing the budget, you should be aware of certain items that especially draw the close attention of agency sleuths. Salaries, consulting fees, and travel allowances rank high among such items. So does any expense that is atypical or unusually large. Your best bet in these circumstances is to forestall the evaluator's questions by making sure those budgetary items are sufficiently detailed. If necessary, footnote your entries and give your verbal justifications at the end of the budget section or on a separate sheet of paper. One of the best ways to predict ahead of time which budgetary items may be touchy is to show your budget draft to the funding program officer. He or she can usually pinpoint the trouble-makers.

Usually the government asks you to break down your budget into direct and indirect costs. Direct costs are those that are exclusively identifiable with the project. They include salaries of the research staff and supplies. Indirect costs are those expenditures not clearly identifiable with the project. To illustrate indirect costs, let's consider a college biology department applying for a government research grant. It is only fair that a share of the college's general administrative costs be applied to the research project. This general overhead includes, for instance, the president's salary, janitorial services, library expenses, building depreciation, and interest costs. Obviously, it would be nearly impossible to say that $2,632 of the president's salary should be applied to the project. That is why there is need for an indirect cost rate.

Express your indirect cost rate in a percentage form (such as 50 percent). It indicates the percentage of your direct payroll (or sometimes another set figure, such as your total direct costs) that you can charge the government to cover your indirect costs. To illustrate: if your direct cost rate is 50 percent and your direct salary and wage expense is $100,000, you can charge the government $50,000 to cover your various unitemized indirect costs.

Your indirect cost rate is determined by the government. If you have dealt with the government before, your institution may already have a predetermined indirect cost rate. (This is usually renegotiated every two or three years). If you haven't yet been assigned a rate, the agency usually gives you a provisional rate that is subject to further revision, either upward or downward. The exact rate percentage is dependent upon a combination of factors, including your type of institution and project. You may even be assigned two rates: one for work performed within the walls of your institution and the other for work performed elsewhere. A typical example would be 50 percent for the intramural and 25 percent for the intermural work.

Some costs can be cleanly categorized as direct or indirect (the project researcher's paycheck is direct and the college president's salary is indirect). Other costs fall into that nebulous area between direct and indirect, as is the case with such items as fringe benefits. In some instances the agency may give you latitude in determining into which category a budgetary item logically falls, so long as you are consistent and don't violate one of the agency's budgetary rules and guidelines.

If the agency doesn't have a standardized budget format and if you don't have a prepared one, you may want to consider using the following eight direct-cost categories:

> Personnel
> Outside services
> Rent
> Utilities
> Equipment
> Supplies
> Travel and meetings
> Miscellaneous expenses

Adjust this eight-category format to suit your specific situation. If your computer costs are extensive, create a separate "Computer" category. Conversely, if your equipment costs are minimal, eliminate that category and list whatever equipment purchases you may have in the "Miscellaneous Expenses" category. (Note: A possible ninth category is "General Reserve" for contingencies. However, while you can use this type of budget category when applying to foundations and corporations, federal agencies prefer that you don't use it.

Each of our eight suggested budget categories will now be discussed independently.

Personnel: If your project is of the service-performing type, this category will probably consume the lion's share of your budget. Personnel expenses can usually be subdivided into two components: salaries and wages, and fringe benefits. If you have to determine the going rate for salaries and wages, check with your personnel office. If this is not feasible, you can usually ascertain the proper pay scales by asking organizations similar to yours about their payments for equivalent positions. If work is to be performed by a salaried employee on a part-time basis, the government usually prefers that you calculate the cost by multiplying the employee's annual salary rate by the percentage of time he will be devoting to the project. Thus, if a project calls for a $30,000-per-year employee to work on the project one day a week for four months, use this calculation: $30,000 \times 20\% \times \frac{4}{12} =$ $2,000." When you pay a professor or academic researcher for summer work, the government frequently asks you to calculate each month's wage in terms of one-ninth of the employee's regular academic annual salary. Generally, giving a worker overtime pay with government grant money is not allowed. Fringe benefits include items such as social-security and unemployment-insurance payments, and health insurance and private retirement contributions. Depending upon the agency's wishes, the fringe benefits either can be broken down precisely or expressed as a percentage of the payroll, in which case they usually vary from around 10 to 20 percent.

Outside Services: In this budget category list the cost of consultants, independent contractors, and professional services, such as those of the bookkeeping and legal variety. These budget items will be scrutinized by the agency to make sure they are both necessary and competitively priced. Should you have donated services (see the discussion on matching grants at the end of this section), list them in this budget category. Be certain that these volunteered services will in fact be delivered or you may find yourself owing the equivalent amount to the government.

Rent: If the rent will be directly paid by your project, it is a direct cost. The same may be true if your institution's accounting department can determine accurately the fair rent value of the space being devoted to your project. Otherwise, the rent will probably be classified as an indirect cost.

Utilities: Under this category fall telephone and telegraph costs —and gas, water, and electricity if they are not part of the rent. The determining factor as to whether utilities are direct or indirect costs is the same as is that for the rent category. Should the expected costs of your telephone message units and/or long-distance calls be excessive, explain and justify the reason.

Equipment: Include in this category equipment that will have a useful life beyond a year or beyond the life of the grant project, whichever comes first. Some agencies refer to such equipment as permanent equipment, and often require that each unit be worth at least $100 or $200 to qualify (otherwise, it would fall into the "supplies" budget category). Typical examples of permanent equipment are office furnishings (desks, chairs, files, cabinets, rugs, curtains, et cetera) and and office equipment (typewriters, photocopy machines, tape recorders, adding machines, electronic data processors, postage meters, et cetera). This equipment may be purchased, leased, rented, borrowed, or donated. Generally, each piece should be itemized individually. To avoid possible subsequent disputes, specify who will take title to each piece of equipment upon completion of the project.

Supplies: If a subcategory in the supplies budget is relatively large (as may be the case for stationery or postage stamps), itemize it individually. Other items (pencils, paper clips, rubber bands, Scotch tape, plain typing and carbon paper, chemicals, et cetera) can be lumped into a single "General Supplies" subcategory. Some agencies call this category "expendable [or consumable] supplies."

Travel and Meetings: To avoid any evaluator's suspicion that you are going on a junket, carefully itemize travel and meeting expenses, especially when they involve out-of-town travel. Avoid combining your expenses as "one trip to New Orleans" if the total exceeds $100. Instead, break down the costs of the air fare, hotel, ground transportation, seminar fee, and so on. Some agencies allow you to charge a per diem rate while others want you to itemize the cost of meals, et cetera. If you are flying, the government usually allows you only the jet economy fare. Check with the funding program office for the allowable car mileage rate (usually about 15¢ per mile).

Miscellaneous Category: This is your catchall basket for relatively small direct-cost budget items that do not fit suitably into other budget categories. Examples may include publications, computer services, insurance, printing, and dues.

On the following pages is a sample one-year budget illustrating some of the pointers described. If any of your budget items (such as legal services) is to be specifically donated or provided gratis by you, indicate the fact with an appropriate footnoted asterisk.

BUDGET

TOTALS

PERSONNEL:

Dr. Jane Doe, Chief Researcher @ $30,000 per year (full time for 12 months)	$30,000	
Dr. John Smith, Research Assistant @ $20,000 per year (50% of time for 12 months)	$10,000	
Dr. Richard Jones, Research Assistant @ $20,000 per year (50% of time for 6 months)	$5,000	
Dr. Timothy Brown, Project Advisor @ $30,000 per year (20% of time for four months)	$2,000	
Secretary @ $10,000 per year (full time for 12 months)	$10,000	
Laboratory Assistant @ $5 per hour (33 hours per week for 52 weeks)	$8,580	
Fringe Benefits (@ 10% of total salaries and wages)	$6,558	
SUBTOTAL: PERSONNEL		$72,138

OUTSIDE SERVICES:

Roberts & Thompson Scientific Consultants (@ $1,000 per month)	$12,000	
Forthson's Chemical Analysis Service (@ $400 per month)	$4,800	
Billings & Billings, patent lawyers	$1,000	
SUBTOTAL: OUTSIDE SERVICES		$17,800

RENT:

Fifteen hundred square feet (@ $9 per square foot per year)	$13,500	$13,500

UTILITIES:

Telephone @ $15 per month	$180	
Local message units (500 calls per month @ 10¢)	$600	
Long-distance calls @ $40 per month	$480	
Gas and electric (part of rent)	$0	
SUBTOTAL: UTILITIES		$1,260

EQUIPMENT:

Purchase of Liston T-204 Apparatus (title of ownership will belong to our organization)	$5,000	
Rental of Gelb Electron Microscope	$2,900	
SUBTOTAL: EQUIPMENT		$7,900

SUPPLIES:
  Chemicals required for project $2,100
  General supplies @ $50 per month $600

  SUBTOTAL: SUPPLIES $2,700

TRAVEL AND MEETINGS:
  Local transportation (taxi, et cetera) @ $40 per month $480
  Chief Researcher's trip to Seattle for the ASA Scientific
    Conference ($175 registration fee, $242 round-trip jet
    economy airfare, $30 ground transportation, $80 for two
    days' lodging and $90 for three days' per diem expenses) $617

SUBTOTAL: TRAVEL AND MEETINGS $1,097

MISCELLANEOUS EXPENSES (OTHER DIRECT COSTS):
  Reference library (purchase of books, trade publications,
    et cetera) $600
  Extra laboratory insurance $440
  Computer time @ $100 per month $1,200
  Printing of final report (50 copies) $200

  SUBTOTAL: MISCELLANEOUS EXPENSES $2,440

TOTAL DIRECT COSTS: $118,835

INDIRECT COSTS:
  40% of salaries and wages exclusive of fringe benefits $28,855

TOTAL DIRECT AND INDIRECT COSTS: $147,690

COST-SHARING ARRANGEMENT:
  Our institution's share (@ 10%) $14,769
  Federal agency's share (@ 90%) $132,921

  TOTAL PROJECT COST $147,690

Cost-sharing is a requirement in a number of federal programs. Basically, cost-sharing means that you and/or some nonfederal funding source must pay for part of the cost of the project. The percentage of this nongovernment contribution varies from program to program and can range from less than 1 percent to over 50 percent.

Congress inserts this cost-sharing requirement into some of its appropriation bills in the hope that a grantee will be more conservative in carrying out a project if the grantee has some form of financial stake in it. When the contribution comes from outside nonfederal sources, it helps assure Congress that the project has local support.

There are two basic types of cost-sharing: "hard" and "soft." "Hard" cost-sharing means that your share must be in the form of cash. "Soft" or "gifts-in-kind" cost-sharing allows you to make noncash contributions such as donated services, equipment, and facilities. If you absorb your indirect costs or agree to pay part of the salary of the researcher, you would be making a "soft" or "gift-in-kind" contribution. Usually the agency and/or the applicable Office of Management and Budget (OMB) Federal Management Circulars specify what types of contributions are allowable for a program.

A free 11-page booklet worth acquiring is *A Guide to Institutional Cost Sharing Agreements for Research Grants and Contracts*. Write:

> Office of Administrative Management
> Public Health Service, 5600 Fishers Lane
> Rockville, Maryland 20852.

Matching funds (and matching "gifts-in-kind") is a concept similar to that of cost-sharing, but slightly different. With matching funds, the government requires you to raise in cash a percentage (usually 50 percent) of the project costs from sources that are not your own or governmental. With matching gifts-in-kind, the contribution can be donated services, property et cetera. Unless Congress and/or the agency specifies that the contribution be in cash, you usually have the choice between "cash" or "gifts-in-kind." The latter type is almost invariably more appealing to the grantee.

A good example of matching funds is the award of money by the National Endowment of the Arts to a symphony orchestra.

The Endowment may, for instance, agree to give the Denver Philharmonic $50,000 when and if the symphony raises $50,000 from local private sources.

The collection of matching funds can be handled in one of two ways, depending upon the agency's policies. The matching funds can be sent to the agency, which in turn transfers them to the grantee along with the agency's matching share. Or the grantee can hold the funds in escrow. Usually there is a time limit on matching funds or gifts-in-kind agreements. Unless the contributions are raised in full by a certain date, the deal is off. Extensions, however, are sometimes given.

Don't think that just because there is a federal matching fund program, all you have to do is to raise your share of the project's cost and the agency will automatically award you the grant. The agency will award you the money only if your project is deemed meritorious.

Who Should Prepare the Application?

Who is the best person to prepare the proposal? For every organization, there is a different answer—but here are some general guidelines:

Ideally, the preparer should be the person who will be carrying out the project because of his or her intimate knowledge of the subject. This ideal person should have four additional qualities: a solid understanding of the relevant grant requirements; negotiating skill (the final details of many grants are settled between the agency and applicant); expertise in preparing budgets; good writing ability.

If this multitalented person is not available (as is the case in most instances), it is usually most effective if the grant-coordinator assumes the centralized authority and responsibility of masterminding the application because of his or her knowledge of the funding program regulations and guidelines. This grant-coordinator should work closely with his or her organization's technical and budgetary experts. If the grant-coordinator happens to lack the needed writing skills, he or she should seek help from someone who has them, especially if the application requires a descriptive narrative section.

Government Information Sources on Preparing Applications

The best source of information on how to prepare an application is the application itself plus its accompanying guidelines prepared by the funding agency. Write for them and they are yours free of charge.

Also write for a free copy of the enabling legislation (see "Copies of Congressional Bills," page 165). After studying this document, you will be better able to pinpoint and perhaps quote in your application (a sound idea) the bill's congressional intent.

Good general instructional information on preparing applications is found in the three free Public Health Service (PHS) booklets described on page 71, in HEW's by-subscription *Grant Administration Manual* (page 73) and in the National Science Foundation's (NSF's) free *Grants for Scientific Research* booklet (page 108).

PHASE FOUR

Submitting Your Application

With few exceptions (such as with the National Science Foundation), government granting agencies have specific final-application deadline dates, occurring at various times throughout the year. If you miss a program's deadline date, your application will either be held for the next review cycle or returned to you. Either way, you've suffered a setback. It is possible for some agencies to waive deadline dates, but the execution of this option is rare.

To be on the safe side, submit your application at least several weeks early because agencies sometimes get backlogged during zero hour. Another bonus for early submission is that it sometimes indicates to the agency official that you are well organized.

How do you determine the deadline date? U.S. Government agencies by law must publish the date in the *Federal Register*. Unfortunately, this announcement sometimes gives no more than a thirty-day notice, too short a period for soundly preparing some applications. The other major published source of deadline dates is the *Catalog of Federal Domestic Assistance*. Generally, it is useful but it, too, has its shortcomings (see page 133).

A funding program officer, on the other hand, usually knows of deadline dates and their revisions well before they are published in the *Federal Register, Catalog of Federal Domestic Assistance,* or any other publication. By cultivating a relationship with the various funding program officers working in your field of interest, you may gain added lead time and a sharp competitive edge.

Avoid delays and even possibly mislaid documents by making sure you submit your application to the right agency office. With some funding programs an agency may require you to send your application to a national-level office, while with other programs the proper office will be a regional-level one.

Also, be sure you submit the required number of copies. The number can vary from one to several, depending on the agency and program.

Theoretically, government grant evaluators shouldn't be influenced by a few typos, misspellings, erasures, and other secretarial foibles, but, being human, they are. Your secretary can also do harm to your grant chances by not double-checking the entire application for missing items such as a signature, by inserting a wrong figure or fact, by forgetting to enclose all relevant material, by misaddressing the envelope, by not using (if necessary) a protective envelope to keep the contents from being mutilated in transit, and by using insufficient postage. The last case may even cause you to miss a deadline, since most government offices automatically return short-postaged mail.

How do you deliver your application? The most frequently employed method is by U.S. mail, first class. Some agencies send acknowledgment letters, others do not. If you want full assurance that your application has been received, mail it via certified mail with a "return-receipt request." For your purposes, this is just as effective and less expensive than is registered mail. A few grantees deliver the application to the appropriate officer by messenger. Others deliver it personally. Should this last method be convenient, it can be a splendid opportunity for reinforcing your growing relationship with the funding program officer.

Now and then you may find yourself in the position of submitting somewhat similar proposals to two different agencies or funding program officers. There is nothing wrong with this action as long as you mention the fact in each of your applications. To wait and see how one application will fare before submitting the other would be putting all your eggs in one basket, a gross mistake in government grant-seeking.

The Review of Your Application

Your final application has been submitted. The responsibility for action now falls into the lap of the agency, which must decide to approve, reject, or defer your funding request.

What happens during this decision-making process? For every agency there is a different process. To give you at least a general idea of what your application goes through, let's examine one possibility:

February 1: You have submitted your final application on or before this date, the programs's official deadline.

February through May: Your application is given a preliminary screening by the agency to make sure it is properly completed and meets the funding program's general guidelines. Upon clearing this initial hurdle, your application starts on its lengthy evaluation journey through the agency's review system. Depending on the agency and program, the degree of sophistication of this system can range from low to high. (The Public Health Service of HEW, the National Science Foundation, and the two Endowments—the Arts and the Humanities—employ some of the better, more refined systems.) If your application goes through a highly sophisticated review process, it may be subjected to a "peer review system." This means it will probably be assigned (either through the mail or in person) to an outside expert or panel of experts for evaluation. These independent and (on the whole) impartial experts, acting either as individuals or as part of a committee, will then rate your application on a point grading system. The identity (and sometimes the opinions) of these experts is usually kept confidential. In addition to being evaluated by the outside experts during this period, your application will probably also be reviewed in depth by the agency's in-house staff.

June through August: The opinions and recommendations of the outside experts and/or the agency's in-house staff will probably now be turned over to a high-level council, committee, or director to make the final go, no-go, or defer-to-a-later-date decision.

September 1: You are notified by first-class mail of the agency's decision.

The above example is hypothetical and is meant only to give you a general indication of what happens during a decision-making process. For specific details on any given program's review system, read the agency's literature and ask the appropriate funding program officer.

In our illustration, the length of time between the deadline date and decision notification is seven months. This is fairly typical—for most grants the period ranges from five to nine months. However, sometimes you may have to wait a year or two. Whatever the period, there is usually no way to speed up the agency's process. Be patient and plan ahead.

While you seldom can expedite the agency's decision-making process, it's a sound idea to keep a running check with the funding program officer on the status and whereabouts of your application as it wends its way through the government's bureaucratic maze. This provides you with partial insurance against the possibility of your application being lost, mislaid, or misfiled—it happens.

Questions Evaluators Ask

True, evaluators are given guidelines to follow in judging the merits of an application. Nonetheless, each of these persons brings to his or her task certain preconceptions and biases, no matter how slight or unintentional these may be. There is therefore no way to predict with complete accuracy how your application is going to be reviewed.

Despite this lack of a precise intelligence report, there are certain basic questions evaluators often ask themselves. Some of the more important queries are given below. Use these questions to see if your proposal has an Achilles' heel.

Have the instructions been followed? [A proposal that does not adhere to the instructions stands out as a prime candidate for early elimination for a host of reasons, including the implication that the applicant lacks interest.]

Does the project correlate with our grant-making policy in terms of the objective? Type of grant? Size of grant? Period? Geographic scope?

Does the application violate any law, such as the Civil Rights Act of 1964. [A federal agency cannot fund a project if it violates a federal, state, or local law.]

Does the application have the required approvals, such as from the A-95 Clearinghouses, if appropriate?

Is the applicant specific as to who will be served? By whom? Where? When? Why? How?

How significant is the need that will be satisfied by the project? Is the timing right for solving the problem?

Does the project duplicate or overlap other programs?

Does the applicant know what others in the field are doing or planning to do? Is the applicant sufficiently current on relevant literature?

Is the applicant aware of the options other than those he is proposing?

Are the applicant's methods well thought out and described? Will these methods work? Are they the best?

Is the timetable realistic? Has the applicant allowed for possible delays?

Are the cost estimates current? Is the budget realistic and sufficiently detailed?

Does the applicant recognize the potential pitfalls and know how to protect the project against them?

Am I familiar with the applicant and the project's idea? [Though this should not be the case, evaluators tend to favor ideas, institutions, and people that are familiar entities.]

Is the individual and/or organization qualified to undertake the project in terms of staff? Leadership? Facilities? Dedication? Enthusiasm? Integrity?

Does the applicant have a sufficient "track record"? [If your organization is new and thus has no track record, emphasize the past accomplishments of your personnel.]

Does the applicant have the proper accreditations? What has the applicant published? What honors has the applicant received?

Are personnel assignments specific and clear? What are each key person's individual qualifications? Is there a chance that some of these people will serve only as window dressing and not actually perform the amount or quality of the work promised?

Does the individual and/or departmental applicant have the full support and cooperation of the overall institution?

What is the quality of the applicant's board of directors or trustees?

Does the applicant have the needed facilities, such as laboratories, library collections, and equipment?

Does the applicant have permission to use needed patents, et cetera?

Does the applicant have the needed contacts and working relationships with other organizations and community leaders to carry out the project successfully?

To what extent will outside consultants and subcontractors be used? Are they qualified? Are their fees and charges reasonable?

What are the chances that the donated services and equipment will not be delivered as promised?

Has the applicant adequately documented all assertions?

Has the applicant furnished names, addresses, and telephone numbers of persons who can verify the applicant's credentials, integrity, dedication, community standing, et cetera? [Use references only if you have first secured the referents' permission.]

Can the project's success be measured and evaluated? How? When?
By whom?

Would an on-site visit now or later be worthwhile?

Will the project have a worthwhile, far-reaching impact beyond
itself?

Will the applicant meet our agency's grant-reporting requirements?

Is the project a good investment for us?

Are we the best source of the needed funds? [Other sources include
other government funding programs, private foundations, corporations, community organizations, and individuals.]

Is there any danger that the project may backfire on my agency—
or on me as an individual? [Take into account the "security
factor" of the government official. If a project runs into a legal
snag or gains unfavorable publicity, for instance, it could
jeopardize the government official's professional reputation or
opportunity for future promotion.]

Why Proposals Fail

Proposals fail for a host of different reasons. A quick glance
at the evaluator's questions will help substantiate this point.
However, to shed some specific light on why proposals do fail,
let's examine a recent survey conducted by Louis E. Masterman. Analyzing some seven hundred applications submitted to
and disapproved by the Public Health Service, he found that:

39% were rejected because of poor planning and/or poorly
prepared applications.

38% were rejected because the applicant did not establish or
have competence.

18% were rejected because the project did not correlate with
the agency's objectives. [This figure would probably be
over 50% in the case of applications submitted by neophyte grant-seekers.]

5% were rejected for miscellaneous reasons.

Postsubmission Negotiation

In many instances an agency may not be willing to fund an otherwise acceptable project because of several small details in your application. Rather than flatly rejecting your project, the agency may try to negotiate with you to change the contended items. Modifications can take any number of forms, including cutting or increasing your project's goals or budget.

Your options are to negotiate—or not to negotiate, in which case you will most likely lose the grant. The first course of action is naturally more prudent. But don't accept the agency's new terms if they compromise your project's integrity or if they alter the project to the point where it becomes a financial or an administrative burden. To take on a grant with undesirable terms is seldom sound, because the quality of your project will probably suffer—and this will hurt your chances of winning future grants, whether from government, foundation, or corporate sources.

If a mutually satisfactory agreement is reached between you and the agency, your application is either redrafted or amended —then approved, usually within a relatively short period.

PHASE SIX

After the Decision Is Made

The official notification of the funding decision will probably arrive by first-class mail, perhaps on a computer-prepared form. If you have the right contacts, you can sometimes learn of the decision before seeing the official written notification—but don't press for this information lest it establish you as pushy in the eyes of the agency.

If the Answer is "Yes"

Your payment usually immediately follows the official written notification. It can be in the form of a Treasury Department check, a letter of credit, a piece of equipment—or a combination of them.

Should you receive a "yes" answer for the same or similar project from two different funding sources (which is unlikely), you will have to choose which of the two grants you would like to receive and then notify both agencies of your decision. Or, you might have them agree to allow you to make adjustments on your applications and thereby possibly undertake two grant programs, concurrently or sequentially.

One of your first tasks is to send a thank-you and acknowledgment letter to the agency. It's good PR. Simultaneously, notify the appropriate people within your organization, community, and field. Also, consider preparing a release for newspapers, trade journals, and other journalistic outlets.

If the Answer is "No"

Don't let an application rejection get you down. If you're not receiving your fair share of rejection notifications, you are probably not applying for as many grants as you should be—and this is probably costing you lost opportunities. Like a home-run hitter, you can strike out a number of times as long as you bring home enough runs—or in your case, grant dollars. If you're afraid to hear the umpire's third-strike call, you'll probably hold back on your power swing or, even worse, avoid batting altogether. Play the percentages. In time you'll connect.

As in the case of receiving an affirmative reply, step 1 after seeing the rejection notification is to write a thank-you letter to the agency. Here is one possible draft:

Dear (funding program officer):

Thank you for reviewing our application for the XYZ program.

We are naturally disappointed by your agency's decision because we believe our project could have served the senior citizens in our community. At the same time, we are fully aware that your limited resources cannot possibly fund all the deserving proposals your agency receives.

I would like very much to keep in steady contact with you. Perhaps in the future we'll have another project that better matches your grant-giving objectives.

Sincerely,

A thank-you letter not only leaves the door open, it also may help you with your other grant-seeking endeavors. Remember, a funding program officer knows and talks with other funding program officers, the ones you may be dealing with on your next grant project.

Try to ascertain why your application was rejected. This will help you with future proposals. The information may even provide you with clues on how to revise your rejected application so it can be approved during the agency's next funding cycle.

The best possible method of determining why your application failed is by asking the funding program officer. You have this right—but use it tactfully. While the funding program officer probably won't tell you who evaluated your proposal and may not be allowed to give you the evaluator's precise comments, the officer can supply you with some specific details. For instance, you may learn which segments of your application caused its downfall. Or you may discover that the fault didn't lie with your application per se. Perhaps some top-level agency official purposely delayed the commitment of the available funds because of presidential pressure.

If the Answer is a "Deferral"

Immediately ask the funding program officer why. If the delay is caused by your application, inquire as to how you should revise it. Also, for your planning purposes, find out how the delay will affect the timing of the decision.

Conducting the Project

Before pushing the start button on the project, carefully restudy all information pertaining to the project, including the grant application, the agency guidelines and regulations, the agency's award notification, and your notes on your conversations with the agency officials. Make sure you understand each small detail. If you do not, double-check with the funding program officer. This precaution may save you headaches later on.

Set up a tight management system. If possible, select one person to authorize all budget expenditures. If you are going to be paid on a cost-reimbursement basis (as would be the case with most state and local government grants), make sure the expenditure receipts are properly and promptly gathered and submitted. New York City recently discovered that it could increase its cash flow by $38 million simply by speeding up the processing of some of its claims against federal and New York State funding programs.

Don't spend or commit a penny until you have the full go-ahead in writing. Many a grantee has prematurely expended money only to discover that the grant was virtually, but not totally approved.

Adhere to the budget. The agency usually gives you some flexibility, but don't take unnecessary liberties. If you are in doubt, inquire first—or you may be liable for the funds yourself.

If a special situation warrants it, agencies are generally willing to change the terms of the grant in midstream. To illustrate: Your budget may be increased in order to research an important subfactor that was not obvious at the onset of the project. Or the agency may give you permission for a change in personnel or work-load assignments. Or you may receive a three-month extension, thereby permitting you to commit funds beyond the original grant period. Should you unilaterally violate the terms of the agreement (budget, methods, et cetera), the grant may be revoked and you will probably end up with a financial or legal disaster.

Auditing is standard practice with government grants. You may even be audited during your project period, especially if many dollars are involved and you haven't previously dealt with the agency. Otherwise, a postaudit is the usual procedure. For either an interim-audit or postaudit, you will have to maintain accurate records from the start. Besides the normal accounting records that prove you have been making expenditures in keeping with the budget provisions, you should also have readily on hand interim project results (if any) and all basic project documents, such as your application and the agency's rules, guidelines, and notification-of-award letter. One centralized file should do the trick.

During the audit, try to have someone on hand who can talk to the auditor in his or her own professional language. Should the auditor find a discrepancy and file a report on it, you have the right to send to the agency your interpretation of the disputed issue. If your case is valid, the agency may overrule the auditor's opinion and side with you. If you think the auditor is right, try to make on-the-spot adjustments of your project to make it compatible with the auditor's wishes. The sooner you rectify the problem, the better off you'll be in the long run.

Besides a visit from an accountant-type auditor, you may receive an on-site visit from the funding program officer or some other professional. Treat these visitors just as you would the accountant: freely open up all your records to them and try to be as honest as possible in your assessment of the project's progress. Follow their suggestions, but only if you consider them rational vis-à-vis your project and your organization. You must judiciously guard your independence against possible government bureaucratic encroachment.

Project Termination

Virtually all government grants require a final report. Sometimes two distinct reports are mandatory: one, a report documenting the administrative and budgetary aspects of the project and the second, reporting on the project results.

The administrative and budget-type report is normally quite easy to prepare if you have maintained good records. Many agencies provide you with a standardized fill-in-the-facts-and-numbers form.

Reporting on the project results is usually a more difficult matter. This kind of report is vital because it will be a key analytical tool in the agency's evaluation of your project. Your report should be brief, specific, and candid. If operational mistakes have been made, they should be freely admitted. Otherwise you run the risk of losing credibility if they are discovered. The same truthful approach should be followed if the project didn't quite accomplish what it set out to do. As long as you've done your best, normally you won't be held legally responsible for failure. The agency usually doesn't expect you to succeed with flying colors every time.

Who should prepare the report? The closer the person(s) is to the project, the better—especially if the project is of a technical nature.

Deadline dates for postproject reports vary from agency to agency, but are usually set for about ninety days after the completion of the project. Whatever the deadline date, don't miss it or you'll have trouble getting future grants. Missing the deadline may also cause a delay in your receiving some cost-reimbursement expenses that are owed you. Be prepared for possible personnel changes. If a key member of the project team is leaving your institution, make sure that a summation of his or her contribution to the project is in your hands in writing before the departure. Trying to acquire this information after a person has joined another institution is taxing at best.

Sometimes the government requires you to have your final report formally published. Depending on the desires of the agency, you may have several publishing options. The usual way is to issue the document yourself in simple typewritten-report format. Perhaps you may elect to do it more elaborately in a brochure or handbook format. Or you may have it published in a professional journal acceptable to the agency. Some final reports have even been full-fledged books.

Generally it's a good idea to keep extra copies on hand, should people in your field request them. There is no reason why you can't charge for these copies.

As far as the government is concerned, you will probably have to keep file copies available for several years, often longer. This is especially true with financial and legal documents because it is not uncommon to receive a postproject audit years later, long after practically everyone has forgotten about the project.

Should you have surplus funds at the end of the project, they must be returned to the agency unless a special arrangement has been made. Any interest that accrues on the government's funding advance must also be returned to the agency, because it is against the law for you to earn income on federal money.

Long Term

As we stress throughout this book, long-term thinking is an essential part of the grant-seeking game. This means not only creating long-range plans of action, but also analyzing current decisions to see how they will affect the future. Stretching a fact in order to win a grant, for instance, may be profitable for year 1, but self-destructive in the years to come because of the negative credibility factor. Once gained, this factor is hard to erase in the minds of funding agency officials.

Tune yourself in to as many solid information sources as your staff and budget will allow. If possible, keep up with the actions of Congress, the rulings and plans of the Executive Branch funding and administrative agencies, and the rulings of the courts. This information will probably give you valuable lead time in discovering grant programs that are coming up. It might even forewarn you of the termination of an existing program, thereby allowing you extra time to find alternative funding sources. Another benefit for keeping abreast is that you may learn of an agency program with surplus year-end dollars. (While such budget surpluses don't guarantee you funding, they certainly increase the odds in your favor.)

If your grant-seeking endeavor is large enough, consider voicing your opinions to legislatures and agency officials before grant programs and regulations become final. While in most instances your opinions will have little impact on the outcome, sometimes they do—and that can make your time investment rewarding.

You can state your case by letter or telephone. Or you can appear before a committee—but be prepared for wasteful hours and sometimes days spent in waiting rooms. Still another option is to speak with congressmen or agency officials in private meetings. These private get-togethers are often more productive than being in front of a committee where the legislators' or officials' minds may be less open to suggestions. Committee meetings, on the other hand, offer better potential for media coverage.

(A well-executed public-relations program can increase the cooperation you will receive from government officials.)

If your grant-seeking endeavor is small (or even if it is large-scale), try to pool your efforts with other individuals and organizations sharing your viewpoint. Collectively you can voice your opinions more powerfully and less expensively than you can individually. The collective approach also increases the chances of your cause receiving media coverage.

Even if your application was turned down, keep in touch with the funding program officer. You may be successful during the next funding round—or the officer may be able to steer you to another funding program. Also try to keep all the other key people (your congressman, et cetera) informed of your doings via letters, meetings, or press coverage, to name a few media. Out of sight, out of mind. People have short memories.

Finally, never stop reassessing the potential value of each individual funding program. Times and circumstances change. Since the resources available to you for seeking grants are limited, you must first assign, then constantly adjust your priorities.

PART TWO
Where the
Money Is

Department of Health, Education, and Welfare (HEW)

Approximately $150 billion will be spent this year by HEW, the undisputed holder of the "U.S. Government Superagency" title. Even the Department of Defense spends less.

It is hard to find an American citizen not directly or indirectly affected by the many public-service programs administered by HEW's 100,000+ employees. In fact, many Americans are helped by HEW from birth to death under a broad range of programs in the fields of health services, income security, education, rehabilitation, to name only a few. Perhaps most important to you, some of these programs create significant funding opportunities.

Don't be discouraged if HEW seems unfathomably vast and complex, because few people have mastered its Byzantine structure. Nevertheless, it is important that you gain at least a general understanding of its basics. To help, we have briefly described the five major HEW operating subdepartments that most concern grant- and contract-seekers:

Education Division
Public Health Service
Office of Human Development
Social and Rehabilitation Service
Social Security Administration

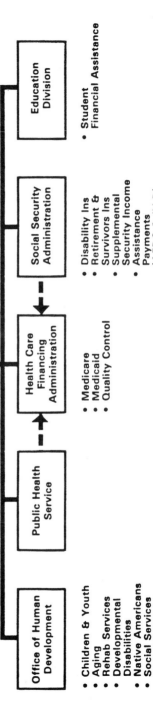

DEPARTMENT OF HEALTH, EDUCATION, AND WELFARE

SECRETARY

OFFICES

ASSISTANT SECRETARIES

- Health Care Financing
- Cash Assistance Payments
- Social Services
- Student Financial Assistance

- Executive Secretariat
- Office for Civil Rights
- Office of General Counsel
- Office of Inspector General

- Legislation
- Public Affairs
- Planning and Evaluation
- Personnel Administration
- Budget and Management

Office of Human Development

- Children & Youth
- Aging
- Rehab Services
- Developmental Disabilities
- Native Americans
- Social Services (Title XX, IV-B)

Public Health Service

Health Care Financing Administration

- Medicare
- Medicaid
- Quality Control

Social Security Administration

- Disability Ins
- Retirement & Survivors Ins
- Supplemental Security Income
- Assistance Payments (AFDC & IV-D)

Education Division

- Student Financial Assistance

Education Division

HEW's Education Division is charged with improving the quality and equality of the American education system in keeping with U.S. Government laws and regulations. It accomplishes its goals through a number of subdivisions, the four main ones being:

Fund for the Improvement of Postsecondary Education
National Centers for Education Statistics
National Institute of Education
Office of Education

The *Fund for the Improvement of Postsecondary Education* (FIPSE) attempts to increase the quality, equality, cost-effectiveness, and innovative nature of college-, graduate-, and postgraduate-level education.

The National Center For Education Statistics collects, analyzes, and disseminates data that might prove useful in the planning, execution, and evaluation of the American educational system.

The *National Institute of Education* (NIE) strives to raise the quality of the education system through applied research and development. NIE's fluctuating budget ($80 million in 1977) is mainly spent to support grants and contracts in the following programs: Basic Skills, Dissemination and Resources, Educational Equality, Education and Work, Finance and Productivity, and School Capacity for Problem-Solving.

The *Office of Education* (OE) is by far the largest and most important component of the Education Division. It provides national leadership as well as giving professional and financial assistance to state and local educational units, public and private educational institutions, and organizations and students. All told, nearly a hundred million students are directly affected by OE's one hundred programs, which cost roughly $7 billion a year. The ultimate beneficiaries include preschoolers, collegians, postdoctoral scholars, vocational trainees, and adult-education students. Funds are spent on student grants and loans, work-study programs, guidance and counseling, erecting and expanding of libraries and laboratories, teacher-training, textbook purchases, handicap-education programs, and a host of other educational areas. The major OE operating units include:

> Bureau of Education for the Handicapped
> Bureau of Occupational and Adult Education
> Bureau of Postsecondary Education
> Bureau of School Systems
> Office of Indian Education
> Office of the Commission of Education

The above-mentioned Bureau of Postsecondary Education administers the Basic Education Opportunity Grant Program for post high-school students. For further information, see "Student Aid," Appendix E.

American Education is the official publication of HEW's Education Division. Once a year this periodical presents a comprehensive and descriptive guide to the various HEW-sponsored educational programs. An annual subscription (ten issues) costs $9.95, but you can receive a free copy of the issue containing the program guide by writing to

> *American Education*
> P.O. Box 9000
> Alexandria, Virginia 22304

For further information on HEW's Education Division, write:

Office of the Assistant Secretary for Education
Department of Health, Education, and Welfare
400 Maryland Avenue, S.W.
Washington, D.C. 20202

Public Health Services (PHS)

PHS's primary mission is to protect and advance the general health of the citizenry. To accomplish its goals, PHS is organized into operating agencies designed to attack specific health problems. Grants and/or contracts are awarded by these six major PHS agencies:

Alcohol, Drug Abuse, and Mental Health Administration
Center for Disease Control
Food and Drug Administration
Health Resources Administration
Health Services Administration
National Institutes of Health

The *Alcohol, Drug Abuse, and Mental Health Administration* (ADAMHA) seeks to furnish national leadership in the war against alcohol and drug abuse and in the treatment and rehabilitation of those afflicted with mental-health problems. In recent years, ADAMHA's annual budget has fluctuated somewhere between one-half and one billion dollars.

The Atlanta-based *Center for Disease Control* (CDC) is charged with preventing and controlling communicable diseases, vector-borne diseases, and certain other preventable health conditions. CDC's major subdivisions are:

Bureau of Epidemiology
Bureau of Health Education
Bureau of Laboratories

Bureau of Smallpox Eradication
Bureau of State Services
Bureau of Training
Bureau of Tropical Diseases
National Institute for Occupational
Safety and Health

The *Food and Drug Administration* (FDA) is responsible for protecting the public against hazards stemming from impure and unsafe foods, drugs, cosmetics, household items, and certain other types of consumer products. The key FDA subdivisions are:

Bureau of Biologics
Bureau of Drugs
Bureau of Foods
Bureau of Medical Devices and Diagnostic Products
Bureau of Radiological Health
Bureau of Veterinary Medicine
National Center for Toxicological Research

The *Health Resources Administration* (HRA) has four major subdivisions: The Bureau of Health Planning and Resources Development attempts to maximize the combined effectiveness of our country's public and private health resources. The Bureau of Health Manpower undertakes and supports programs to increase the quality and number of personnel in the health field. The National Center for Health Services Research strives to coordinate and promote the effectiveness of research and program evaluation within PHS and the health-services field in general. The National Center for Health Statistics collects, analyzes, and disseminates data that might be useful in the planning, development, and administration of the nation's health resources. For a free subscription to HRA's monthly *Health Resources News,* write:

> Health Resources News
> Human Resources Administration
> Public Health Services
> HEW
> 5600 Fishers Lane
> Rockville, Maryland 20852

The *Health Services Administration* (HSA) strives to improve the delivery of the nation's health services. One of HSA's other duties is the provision of medical care for a specific population group such as American Indians, Alaskan natives, mothers and children, migrant workers, and federal employees. HSA also advises Social Security and certain other federal programs on medical-care standards. The four chief HSA subdivisions are:

> Bureau of Community Health Services
> Bureau of Medical Service
> Bureau of Quality Assurance
> Indian Health Service

The *National Institutes of Health* (NIH) attempts to improve the health of the American population by conducting and supporting research into the causes, prevention, and cure of diseases by facilitating biomedical communications, by supporting research training and resources, and by administering U.S. Government standards for biological products sold across state lines. NIH has a number of operating agencies, most with self-descriptive titles (see below). Of these NIH components, the Cancer and the Heart and Lung Institutes account for over half of NIH's $2 billion annual budget.

Clinical Center
Division of Computer Research and Technology
Division of Research Grants (administrative function)
Division of Research Services
Division of Research Sources
Fogarty International Center
National Cancer Institute
National Eye Institute
National Heart and Lung Institute
National Institute of Allergy and Infectious Diseases
National Institute of Arthritis, Metabolism and
    Digestive Diseases
National Institute of Child Health and Human
    Development
National Institute of Dental Research
National Institute of Environmental Health Sciences
National Institute of General Medical Sciences
National Institute of Neurological and Communicative
    Disorders and Stroke
National Institute on Aging
National Library of Medicine

Few government agencies can rival the Public Health Services in the preparation of useful publications for grant- and contract-seekers. As a matter of fact, their publications are so filled with general government grant- and contract-seeking information that it would be worth your while to acquire them even if you're not seeking funds from PHS, let alone from HEW. The following publications are available free by writing to:

Director, NIH
Bethesda, Maryland 20014

PHS Grants Policy Statement: A 24-page booklet explaining in layman's language the grant-application process and terminology.

NIH Guide for Grants and Contracts: A 33-page pamphlet giving general instruction on the initiation, award, and administration of NIH-funded research contracts.

A Guide to the NIH Research Contracting Process: A 25-page primer for neophyte NIH contract-seekers.

Another publication, *Profiles of Grant Programs,* provides overview descriptions of the PHS health programs. For a copy, send $1.55 to:

Profiles of Grant Programs
Superintendent of Documents
U.S. Government Printing Office
Washington, D.C. 20402

Office of Human Development (OHD)

OHD funds approximately one billion dollars' worth of programs that benefit selected population groups with specific needs. These target groups include children and youth, the elderly, rural residents, American Indians, Alaskan natives, and the physically and mentally disadvantaged.

The following OHD subunits (each with a self-descriptive title) administers sizable grant programs:

Administration on Aging (AOA)
Office of Child Development (OCD)—Head Start, et cetera
Office of Developmental Disabilities
Office of Native American Programs (ONAP)
Office of Youth Development (OYD)
Rehabilitation Services Administration (RSA)

For a free copy of OHD's annual report describing its various programs—and for information on OHD in general—write:

The Office of the Assistant Secretary
for Human Development
HEW
330 Independence Avenue, S.W.
Washington, D.C. 20201

Social and Rehabilitation Service (SRS)

SRS provides monetary help and medical care to families, dependent children, and other persons who are disabled, handicapped, or financially incapacitated. In carrying out its mission, SRS annually dispenses roughly $10 billion, mostly to state and local governments.

SRS's key subdivisions from the grant- or contract-seekers' point of view are the Medical Services Administration and the Assistance Payments Administration (APA). The latter administers income maintenance programs such as Aid to Families with Dependent Children (AFDC).

One of SRS's major responsibilities is administering the multi-billion-dollar Title XX program. Basically, Title XX calls for the awarding by the Federal government of block grants to states for use in welfare and other poverty-related programs.

For a free copy of SRS's *Grants Administration Policies* 53-page booklet—and for further information specifically relating to SRS and its programs, including Title XX—write:

Office of the Administrator
Social and Rehabilitation Service
HEW
330 C Street, S.W.
Washington, D.C. 20201

Social Security Administration (SSA)

SSA dispenses over two-thirds (about $100 billion annually) of HEW's total budget. This money goes primarily to retired workers (or their surviving spouses and child dependents) who have contributed to the Social Security trust fund through payroll deductions. SSA also administers two other major programs: Medicare, for the aged; and supplemental income, for the aged, blind, and disabled. While the lion's share of the funds are dispersed directly to individuals, some dollars are dispersed to public and private organizations (in the form of grants and contracts) for such purposes as researching the poverty problems of the aged.

For specific information, write:

> Office of the Commissioner of
> Social Security
> HEW
> 6401 Security Boulevard
> Baltimore, Maryland 21235

Important Hew Publications

HEW has a number of general publications designed to aid grant- and contract-seekers. The three most important ones are:

Grants Administration Manual: This comprehensive looseleaf instructional guide is a virtual necessity for anyone deeply involved in seeking grants or contracts from HEW—and perhaps from the Federal government in general. It defines and describes in detail most of the administrative and financial policies and procedures established by HEW and its subunits. For a copy and its updates, mail $17.50 to:

> Grants Administration Manual
> Superintendent of Documents
> U.S. Government Printing Office
> Washington, D.C. 20402

Financial Assistance by Geographic Area: There are ten books in this annual series, one for each HEW region. Each book tells you how HEW allotted its domestic-assistance program dollars for the preceding fiscal year. You'll learn not only how much of HEW's funds were obligated in each state, county, congressional district, and city; you will also see the names of the recipients and the exact dollar amount obligated to them by each HEW program. If you can establish your need for the data contained in the books, you can receive a free copy by writing the comptroller of the appropriate HEW regional office.

How to Do Business with DHEW: You can obtain a free copy of this 41-page pocket-sized primer by writing to the Office of the Secretary (see address below).

Further Information

For information on HEW in general, write:

> The Office of the Secretary of
>   Health, Education, and Welfare
> 330 Independence Avenue, S.W.
> Washington, D.C. 20210

But in most cases, because of the somewhat decentralized HEW organizational structure, you are better off telephoning or mailing your inquiry to the appropriate regional office listed below. (See map on page 146 for regional boundaries):

> HEW REGION I
> John F. Kennedy Federal Building
> Boston, Massachusetts 02203
> (617) 223–6831
>
> HEW REGION II
> 26 Federal Plaza
> New York, New York 10007
> (212) 264–4600

HEW REGION III
3535 Market Street
Philadelphia, Pennsylvania 19101
(215) 597–6492

HEW REGION IV
50 Seventh Street N.E.
Atlanta, Georgia 30323
(404) 526–5817

HEW REGION V
300 South Wacker Drive
Chicago, Illinois 60606
(312) 353–5160

HEW REGION VI
1114 Commerce Street
Dallas, Texas 75202
(214) 749–3396

HEW REGION VII
601 East 12th Street
Kansas City, Missouri 64106
(816) 374–3436

HEW REGION VIII
1961 Stout Street
Denver, Colorado 80202
(303) 837–3373

HEW REGION IX
50 Fulton Street
San Francisco, California 94102
(415) 556–6746

HEW REGION X
1321 Second Avenue
Seattle, Washington 98101
(206) 442–0420

Finally, if you plan to be dealing actively with HEW, you may want to obtain the comprehensive telephone directory of the Department of Health, Education, and Welfare. For details, write:

> HEW Telephone Directory
> Superintendent of Documents
> U.S. Government Printing Office
> Washington, D.C. 20402

Other U.S. Government Agencies

The preceding section described HEW, the largest single source of funds for grant- and contract-seekers (the latter is described in Appendix H). This section briefly outlines the principal funding thrusts of the other Executive Branch departments and independent agencies administering sizable grant and/or contract programs.

Action

Grant money is available to help nonprofit organizations set up volunteer programs that help solve poverty-related problems of communities here and abroad. ACTION's principal operational units are Volunteers in Service to America (VISTA), The Peace Corps, Special Volunteer Programs (SVP), Foster Grandparent Program, Retired Senior Volunteer Programs (RSVP), Senior Companion Program, Service Corps of Retired Executives (SCORE), Active Corps of Executives (ACE), University Year for Action (UYA), and National Student Volunteer Program (NSVP). For details, contact the appropriate ACTION office, or:

The Office of the Director
ACTION
806 Connecticut Avenue, N.W.
Washington, D.C. 20525
(202) 393–3111

Agriculture, U.S. Department of (USDA)

USDA spends some $10 billion annually in carrying out its broad range of programs, which include consumer protection and education, data collection and dissemination, trade inspection and regulation, farmer income maintenance, rural development, environmental conservation, surplus disposal, and agricultural research. A sizable amount of USDA's budget is awarded to grant- and contract-seekers. For special details or general information, contact the appropriate USDA office, or:

Office of the Secretary of Agriculture
14th Street and Independence Avenue, S.W.
Washington, D.C. 20250
(202) 655–4000

Appalachian Regional Commission (ARC)

An independent agency, ARC provides several hundred million dollars annually in grants and other forms of assistance for economic and social development projects in the 13-state, 397-county Appalachian Mountain region. Principal recipients are state and local governments and nonprofit organizations. For details, contact:

Office of the Federal Cochairman
Appalachian Regional Commission
1666 Connecticut Avenue, N.W.
Washington, D.C. 20235
(202) 967–4828

Commerce, U.S. Department of (DOC)

The Department of Commerce is responsible for fostering and promoting America's environmental development and technological advancement. Its annual budget of approximately $4 billion is principally spent (some for grants and contracts) in the following program areas:

Economic Development Assistance: The Economic Development Administration (EDA) and the Regional Action Planning Commissions (RAPC) invest several hundred million dollars a year in aiding low-income and high-unemployment areas by financially assisting private enterprises and by creating new job opportunities.

Promotion of Industry and Commerce: This Department of Commerce arm spends over $100 million annually in helping American businesses better compete here and abroad, in helping minority business enterprises, and in increasing the number of tourists visiting the United States.

Science and Technology: About a half billion dollars is spent by the National Oceanic and Atmospheric Administration in researching and conserving domestic and global natural resources such as the ocean and atmosphere. About another half billion dollars is invested in the Maritime Administration to maintain the U.S. merchant marine and to support maritime subsidies. Nearly $100 million is also spent in each of these two areas: fire prevention and control; science and technical research.

For specific details on the Department of Commerce and its various programs, contact the appropriate DOC office, or:

Office of the Secretary of Commerce
14th Street and Constitution Avenue, N.W.
Washington, D.C. 20230
(202) 783–9200

Community Services Administration (CSA)

The several-hundred-million dollar budget of this independent agency assists the poor, primarily through two programs. Its Community Action Program strives to improve the economic and social lot of some 25 million poor people by working through approximately 900 community action agencies operating in all 50 states. CSA's Economic Development Program attempts to build economic strength in deprived communities and areas by funding Community Development Corporations. The poor are also aided through three other programs: Community Food and Nutrition, Senior Opportunities and Services for the Elderly, and Energy-and-Weatherization. Of the Programs mentioned, the Economic Development Program disperses the most dollars to grant-and-contract seekers. For specific details or general information, contact the appropriate CSA office or:

> Office of Public Affairs
> Community Services Administration
> 1200 Nineteenth Street, N.W.
> Washington, D.C. 20506
> (202) 254–5590

Defense, U.S. Department of (DOD)

Roughly $100 billion a year is spent by the Department of Defense in providing for the military security of the United States. Much of this money is awarded in contracts to public and private organizations for research, development, and goods and services of such diversity that it would be impossible for this book to list them. The best single over-all information source is *Commerce Business Daily* (see page 161). Also contact the appropriate DOD office, or:

Office of the Secretary of Defense
The Pentagon
Washington, D.C. 20301
(202) 545–6700

Energy Research and Development Administration (ERDA)

ERDA's annual budget of approximately $3 billion is spent for the research and development of sources of energy that will help make the United States self-sufficient. Grants and/or contracts are awarded for nuclear, geothermal, solar, fossil, and synthetic-fuel research and development programs. For specific details or general information, contact the appropriate ERDA office, or:

Office of the Administrator
ERDA
20 Massachusetts Avenue, N.W.
Washington, D.C. 20545
(202) 376–4000

There is speculation that ERDA will cease to exist as an independent agency. In such a case, its functions will be transferred to another federal agency.

Environmental Protection Agency (EPA)

EPA's mission is to protect the environment of the United States, especially in terms of air and water pollution. Its annual budget of nearly $5 billion helps finance construction projects and funds leadership, training, public education, governmental and industrial coordination, research and development, and enforcement activities. State and local governments are the primary recipients of EPA's grants and contracts, though nonprofit organizations do receive some of the money. For specific details or general information, contact the appropriate EPA office, or:

> Office of the Administrator
> EPA
> 401 M Street, S.W.
> Washington, D.C. 20460
> (202) 755–2673

Equal Employment Opportunity Commission (EEOC)

Besides performing its litigation duties, EEOC makes funds available to states and to local government agencies to help them pay for research and other mutual-interest projects involving fair employment practices. For specific details or general information, contact the appropriate EEOC office, or:

> Office of the Chairman
> Equal Employment Opportunity Commission
> 2401 East Street, N.W.
> Washington, D.C. 20506
> (202) 634–7040

Federal Energy Administration (FEA)

While ERDA specializes in the research and developmental aspects of solving the energy crisis, FEA addresses itself more to immediate solutions of the energy-shortage problem. Its $100 million-plus annual budget is used to analyze, conserve, regulate, and develop energy sources. Some of its money is given to state and local governments in the form of technical and program support. For specific details or general information, contact the appropriate FEA office, or:

Office of the Administrator
Federal Energy Administration
Pennsylvania Avenue and 12th Street, N.W.
Washington, D.C. 20461
(202) 961–6216

There is speculation that FEA will cease to exist as an independent agency. In that case, its functions will be transferred to another federal agency.

General Services Administration (GSA)

GSA is the "office manager" of the U.S. Government. Among its many duties, GSA operates and arranges for the construction of building facilities, buys and manages transportation vehicles and communication supplies, and procures and distributes office supplies. These activities produce opportunities for contract-seekers.

GSA also administers programs that benefit grant-seekers. One is the Federal Information Center system (see page 140). Others are the excess- and surplus-property disposal programs.

Falling under the term "excess property" are items no longer needed by a particular federal agency. GSA notifies the other federal agencies of the availability of these goods. If any federal agency (or, sometimes, its grantees or contractors) needs the excess property, GSA arranges for the free transfer of ownership. In a typical year, close to $1 billion of excess property changes hands.

In the event that no one claims the excess property, it becomes classified as "surplus property." GSA can donate these goods to subnational governmental units and nonprofit public-service organizations—or GSA can sell the property outright to private sources (for instance: an army-surplus-store wholesaler).

For specific details or general information on the excess-

and surplus-property programs, contact the appropriate GSA office, or:

> Office of the Commissioner
> Federal Supply Service
> General Services Administration
> 1941 Jefferson Davis Highway
> Arlington, Virginia 20406
> (703) 557–1139

Housing and Urban Development, U.S. Department of (HUD)

The underlying mission of HUD is to help low- and moderate-income citizens of urban communities by contracting for and supporting programs that will develop or improve their housing, living environment, and economic opportunities. In an average year, tens of billions of dollars are authorized to fund a number of program areas.

The Community Development Block Grant Assistance Program is the most important to state and local governments. It gives several billion dollars a year in nonmatching formula grants to fund a wide range of community improvement programs such as Neighborhood Development Programs, Model Cities, water and sewer projects, parks and recreational space, and neighborhood and senior-citizen centers. The subnational governments are given a reasonable degree of flexibility in selecting the specific projects, as long as those projects meet with general community approval.

Other ways in which HUD fulfills its over-all objectives is by furnishing financial and technical assistance to public and private housing and new community programs, by providing insurance (mortgage, flood, crime, disaster, et cetera), by administering historic-preservation and housing-discrimination laws and regulations, by regulating interstate-land and mobile-home sales, and by helping communities better plan for the future.

HUD prepares a number of useful publications for grant- and contract-seekers. One is the weekly *HUD Newsletter* (12.75 per year), designed to keep you abreast of the various HUD program developments. Another is the *Hud Challenge* ($19.90 per year); each issue of this monthly magazine focuses on a specific HUD program area. Subscriptions for either of these publications may be obtained from:

> Superintendent of Documents
> U.S. Government Printing Office
> Washington, D.C. 20402.

Also worth obtaining are the informative *Guidelines for Submitting Proposals* booklet (useful to any government grant- or contract-seeker) and the *Selected Information Sources for Urban Specialists* publication. Both are available free directly from HUD (see address below).

For specific details or general information about HUD, contact the appropriate HUD office, or:

Office of the Secretary of Housing and Urban Development
451 7th Street, S.W.
Washington, D.C. 20401
(202) 655–4000

Inter-American Foundation

Somewhere in the neighborhood of $25 million a year is awarded to support projects that facilitate positive social change in Latin America and the Caribbean. For the specifics, contact:

> Office of the President
> Inter-American Foundation
> 1515 Wilson Boulevard
> Rosslyn, Virginia 22209
> (703) 841–3800

Interior, U.S. Department of the (DOI)

Most of the Interior Department's $2- to $3-billion annual budget is used for the day-to-day operation of maintaining and conserving five hundred million acres of public land (national parks, land and water resources, hydroelectric power and flood-control dam systems, et cetera) and for carrying out its assigned programs (land reclamation, water research, outdoor recreation, fish and wildlife management, geological surveys, mining safety, Indian and territorial affairs, the census, et cetera). A small but notable portion of this money is given out in the form of contracts and grants. For specific details or general information, contact the appropriate DOI office, or:

> Office of the Secretary of the Interior
> 18th and C Streets, N.W.
> Washington, D.C. 20240
> (202) 343–1100

Justice, U.S. Department of

Of the Department's $2 billion annual budget, about one-third is spent by the Law Enforcement Assistance Administration (LEAA), the division of the Justice Department that most concerns grant-seekers. This LEAA money is channeled (usually in block grants) to states and local governments for the purpose of providing financial and technical aid for such programs as crime reduction, prisoner rehabilitation, and law-officer training. Prospective grant-recipients should obtain a subscription to the ten-times-a-year *LEAA Newsletter,* which gives information on new grant programs and awards. Also worth obtaining is the annual *LEAA Guide for Discretionary Grant Programs.* Both are available free from LEAA. (Use the Department of Justice address below.)

Besides its LEAA duties, the Justice Department is in charge of a number of other important governmental bodies, including the FBI, the Bureau of Prisons, the Drug Enforcement Administration, the Immigration and Naturalization Service, and a host of operating divisions: Antitrust, Civil, Civil Rights, Criminal, Land and Natural Resources, and Tax.

For specific details or general information, contact the appropriate Department of Justice office, or:

> Office of the Attorney General
> U.S. Department of Justice
> 10th Street and Constitution Avenue, N.W.
> Washington, D.C. 20530
> (202) 737–8200

Labor, U.S. Department of (DOL)

The primary objectives of the U.S. Department of Labor (DOL) are to improve the welfare, employment opportunities, and working conditions of the American labor force. To accomplish these goals, the Department of Labor spends roughly $20 billion annually, conducting or funding a number of programs: unemployment insurance, employment services, training, and work safety, to name a few. The Department is divided into five major domestic divisions:

> Employment and Training Administration
> Bureau of Labor Statistics
> Employment Standards Administration
> Labor-Management Services Administration
> Occupational Safety and Health Administration

Of these five divisions, the Employment and Training Administration (ETA) is by far the largest dispenser of federal funds—to the tune of some $15 billion a year. ETA's principal subunits are:

Office of Comprehensive Employment Development (OCED)
United States Employment Service (USES)
Unemployment Insurance Service (UIS)

The mandate of the first subunit, OCED, is to help provide employment and training opportunities for disadvantaged, unemployed, and underemployed persons.

OCED's chief vehicle is the Comprehensive Employment and Training Act (CETA), which established, among other programs, the Comprehensive Manpower Services, Emergency Job Programs, Job Corps (for youth), National Indian and Native American Program, National Migrant Worker Program, National Older Worker Program, National On-The-Job Training Program, and Public Employment Programs.

CETA authorizes OCED to give a couple of billion dollars a year in block grants to some five hundred eligible "prime sponsors." These prime sponsors are state and local governments with populations of more than a hundred thousand—and occasionally to smaller local governmental units (or combinations of them) that have unusually acute unemployment problems in the judgment of the Secretary of Labor.

A prime sponsor can use the funds to help finance a wide variety of projects of its own choosing as long as they meet the general CETA guidelines. Moreover, the prime sponsor is encouraged to subcontract CETA grant money to local groups, especially to Community Based Organizations (CBOs). This decentralization approach is in keeping with the New Federalism philosophy.

CETA funds are allocated on a formula basis that takes into account the prime sponsor's allotment for the previous fiscal year, its unemployment rate, and the number of adults in low-income families.

Another major OCED program area is the Work Incentive Program (WIN), which is coadministered with HEW. Its aim is to help recipients of the Aid to Families with Dependent Children (AFDC) program find gainful employment, thereby eliminating or reducing their need for AFDC funds. Consequently, the WIN program can increase a family's income and self-esteem while at the same time saving the U.S. Government money.

While OCED is certainly the most important subunit of the Employment and Training Administration as far as a grant-seeker is concerned, there are at least two other ETA subunits that are significant forces in themselves. The United States Employment Service (USES), among its other functions, gives financial aid to state governments to operate local public employment offices. The Unemployment Insurance Service (UIS) advises the state employment security agencies on policies concerning the federal-state unemployment insurance and income maintenance programs.

The Department of Labor scores a good mark in the preparation of useful publications designed for the grant- and contract-seeker. The monthly *Interchange* newsletter keeps you up to date on CETA-related programs. *Community Based Organizations* is a guide for CBOs. Both publications are available free from the Department of Labor (see address below).

For specific details or for general information, contact the appropriate DOL office, or:

Office of the Secretary of Labor
3rd Street and Constitution Avenue, N.W.
Washington, D.C. 20210
(202) 393–2420

National Aeronautics and Space Administration (NASA)

NASA's several-billion-dollar annual budget funds such celebrated projects as manned space flights and planetary probes. The agency extensively awards research contracts and grants to outside organizations, especially to colleges and research institutions. But rather than being "blue sky" in nature, the funded projects almost always relate directly to NASA's specific aerospace research and exploration missions. Some funds, however, are available for such indirect activities as helping schools, museums, and civic organizations develop aerospace educational programs.

Though not as large as it was during its mid-60s heyday, NASA is almost certainly here to stay. It has many loyal supporters in Congress, including Senators John Glenn and Harrison Schmitt, two former astronauts.

In addition to continuing its traditional programs, NASA will be branching out into new fields. Two relatively new program directions, for example, are aerospace environmental preservation and energy research.

For specific details or general information, contact the appropriate NASA office, or:

> Office of the Administrator
> National Aeronautics and Space Administration
> 400 Maryland Avenue, S.W.
> Washington, D.C. 20546
> (202) 755–3905

Nuclear Regulatory Commission (NRC)

While NRC spends the bulk of its $200 million annual budget internally in performing its nuclear energy licensing, regulation, safety, and planning duties, it does award some contracts. These contracts are principally for research projects that help the commission perform its statutory functions. For specific details or general information, contact:

> Office of the Chairman
> Nuclear Regulatory Commission
> 1717 H Street, N.W.
> Washington, D.C. 20555
> (301) 492–7000

Small Business Administration (SBA)

The Small Business Administration has an annual business-loan and investment fund of several hundred million dollars earmarked to help small businesses as well as state and local development organizations. This money is dispensed principally in the form of direct and guaranteed grants.

SBA also has a $100 million disaster loan fund to help small businesses recover from catastrophies. They include natural ones (floods, et cetera), forced relocation (due to an urban development project, et cetera), and product disasters (such as discovering a toxic ingredient in a food product).

SBA also helps small businesses by providing management counseling services and by helping them get a fair share of federal contracts and surplus property.

For a copy of form 115-A that lists the free SBA publications —and for other specific details and general information—contact the appropriate SBA office or:

Office of the Administrator
Small Business Administration
1441 L Street N.W.
Washington, D.C. 20416
(202) 653-6600

Smithsonian Institution

Each year the Smithsonian Institution spends about $100 million to underwrite its extensive museum, research, scientific-information exchange, and public-education programs. Most of these funds are used for internal operations, but some money is awarded in the form of contracts and grants to organizations and individuals carrying out projects that support or relate to the objectives of the Smithsonian Institution.

Under the broad Smithsonian Institution umbrella are too

many distinguished units and programs to list here. Some of the best known are the Anacostia Neighborhood Museum, Archives of American Art, Cooper-Hewitt Museum, Freer Gallery of Art, Hirshhorn Museum, Kennedy Center for the Performing Arts, National Air and Space Museum, National Collection of Fine Arts, National Gallery of Art, National Museum of History and Technology, National Museum of Natural History, National Portrait Gallery, National Zoological Park, and the *Smithsonian Magazine*.

For specific details or general information, contact the appropriate Smithsonian Institution office, or:

> Office of the Secretary
> Smithsonian Institution
> 1000 Jefferson Drive, S.W.
> Washington, D.C. 20560
> (202) 628–4422

State, U.S. Department of

The billion-dollar-a-year State Department establishment is responsible for formulating and executing (under the direction of the President) the foreign policy of the United States.

Of particular interest to fund-seekers is the State Department's Bureau of Educational and Cultural Affairs. This subunit spends roughly $50 million a year in promoting "people to people" understanding between America and other nations. This involves the exchange of students, educators, and various leaders; and the sending of American athletes and performing artists abroad to coach or perform. For information relating to this program, contact the Office of the Secretary for Educational and Cultural Affairs at the State Department address listed below.

Another major State Department funding area is the Agency for International Development (AID), which makes loans and provides technical assistance to developing nations. Key program areas include food and nutrition, population planning and health, education and human resources. Procurement sources for AID financed goods and services are normally selected through competitive bidding. Information on projects proposed for AID financing is publicized in the Commerce Business Daily and AID's Small Business Publication. AID also has another program that might be of interest to you: Overseas Relief Grants. Under this program, AID provides eligible American-managed relief, social, voluntary, and religious organizations with direct financial assistance in the form of grants, contracts, medical supplies, food, or excess property to help foreign victims of both disasters and certain socioeconomic problems. To be eligible for Overseas Relief Grants, you must first register with AID. For further information on this or any other AID program, contact the appropriate AID office, or:

> Office of the Administrator
> Agency for International Development
> 320 21st Street, N.E.
> Washington, D.C. 20523
> (202) 655–4000

For other State Department information, contact the appropriate office, or:

> The Office of the Secretary of State
> 2201 C Street N.W.
> Washington, D.C. 20520
> (202) 655–4000

Tennessee Valley Authority (TVA)

TVA awards a number of contracts for research, construction, and goods and services to help provide nuclear and hydro-electric power, flood control, watersheds, and environmental protection for parts of the seven states within its jurisdiction. Other program areas include fertilizer research and regional economic development. For specific details or general information, contact the appropriate TVA office, or:

> Office of the Chairman
> Tennessee Valley Authority
> New Sprankle Building
> Knoxville, Tennessee 37902
> (615) 637–0101

Transportation, U.S. Department of (DOT)

DOT's $15 billion plus budget goes to developing a safe, cost-effective, and convenient national transportation system—and to fund the operations of its key administrative divisions:

> Federal Aviation Administration
> Federal Highway Administration
> Federal Railroad Administration
> National Highway Traffic Safety Administration
> Saint Lawrence Seaway Development Corporation
> Urban Mass Transportation Administration
> U.S. Coast Guard

Funds in the form of contracts and/or grants are readily available from most of the above subunits. For instance, the Federal Highway Administration doles out billions of dollars a year (principally to state governments) to improve the national highway system; the Urban Mass Transportation Administration grants about $70 million a year to public and private organizations for research and demonstration projects; and the Federal Aviation Administration awards several hundred million dollars per year in grants and contracts to develop and improve public airports.

For special details or general information, contact the appropriate DOT office, or:

Office of the Secretary of Transportation
400 7th Street, S.W.
Washington, D.C. 20590
(202) 426-4000

Treasury, U.S. Department of the

The Treasury Department's diverse duties include overseeing the Internal Revenue, Customs, and Secret Services—as well as directing an assortment of bureaus: Mint, Engraving and Printing, Public Debt, and Alcohol, Tobacco and Firearms. The department also makes sizable revolving seasonal loans to the financially stricken City of New York. But of most relevance to the grant- and contract-seeker is the Treasury Department-administered General Revenue Sharing program.

Under the General Revenue Sharing (GRS) program, the Treasury Department will give over $6 billion each year through September 30, 1980, to some 39,000 eligible state and local governments. The underlying objective of GRS is to decentralize the decision-making authority on how some of the federal funds should be spent.

GRS funds are allocated as follows: one-third to state governments, and two-thirds to local governments (counties, cities, towns, villages, boroughs, townships, Indian tribes, and Alaskan Native villages). A state government is given few restrictions on how the money may be spent. A local government, on the other hand, is somewhat more restricted. It can spend the money only for capital expenditures it normally finances, and for operating and maintenance expenditures that fall into certain broad categories: environmental protection, financial administration, health, libraries, public safety, public transportation, recreation and social services for the poor or aged.

Neither state nor local governments are permitted to use

GRS money to meet federal matching-fund requirements, to finance discriminatory programs, or to fund projects that conflict with existing federal, state, or local rules and procedures. In addition, local governments may not use the money for direct welfare payments, for general-education operating expenses (though construction and equipment expenses are permitted), for general administrative expenses such as the mayor's salary, voter registration, or lobbying.

The money each state and local government receives is generally determined by a three-criteria formula: population, per capita income, and the effort the governmental unit expends in meeting its tax needs. The statistics used in the calculation are based upon data collected by the Bureau of the Census.

The Treasury Department is currently revising old and issuing new instructional publications on its GRS program. For a list of these publications, and for specific or general information on the General Revenue Sharing program, contact the appropriate GRS office, or:

> Office of the Director of Revenue Sharing
> Department of the Treasury
> 15th Street and Pennsylvania Avenue, N.W.
> Washington, D.C. 20220
> (202) 393–6400

United States Information Agency (USIA)

USIA is the international "public relations" arm of the American government. It spends over $200 million a year promoting a favorable image of America abroad via the electronic media (Voice of America, motion pictures, et cetera), print media, information centers, lectures, conferences, exhibitions, and foreign press relations. All these activities have created and will continue to create funding opportunities for contract-seekers. For specific details or general information, contact the appropriate office, or:

Office of the Director
United States Information Agency
1750 Pennsylvania Avenue, N.W.
Washington, D.C. 20547
(202) 655–4000

Veterans Administration (VA)

The VA's mission is to aid veterans and their surviving dependents. To accomplish this objective, the VA spends about $19 billion a year conducting a variety of programs assisting eligible individuals. These programs include medical care, counseling, compensation and pension, education and rehabilitation, loan guarantees, life insurance, and death-related services.

While the VA spends most of its budget internally, it does award contracts to public and private organizations for outside goods and services, especially in the areas of medical research, construction, and training.

For specific details or general information, contact the appropriate VA office, or:

Office of the Administrator of Veterans Affairs
Veterans Administration
810 Vermont Avenue, N.W.
Washington, D.C. 20420
(202) 393–4120

Other Federal Sources

In this and the preceding section, we have briefly described the cabinet-level departments, independent agencies, and commissions that have historically proven to be the best funding sources. We would also like to bring to your attention the following independent agencies:

Export-Import Bank of the United States
Farm Credit Administration
Federal Deposit Insurance Corporation
Federal Home Loan Bank Board
Federal Reserve System
National Credit Union Administration
Overseas Private Investment Corporation
Pension Benefit Guaranty Corporation
Railroad Retirement Board

While these agencies are not significant contract or grant-funding sources, they do provide some type of major financial aid such as loans, loan guarantees, and insurance to particular public and private sectors (for example, the banking industry). There are another several dozen independent agencies that we have chosen not to mention because they are zero- or low-probability sources of financial aid. Essentially, these agencies are regulatory (Federal Trade Commission, et cetera) or administrative (OMB, et cetera) in nature.

Still other potential sources of financial and/or guidance assistance are certain federal commissions, boards, committees, and foundations. These include:

Advisory Board on National Parks, Historic Sites, Buildings, and Monuments
Board of Foreign Scholarships
Citizens' Advisory Committee on Environmental Quality
Citizens' Advisory Council on the Status of Women
Commission on Presidential Scholars
Committee for Purchase from the Blind and Other Severely Handicapped
Delaware River Basin Commission
Federal Advisory Council on Regional Economic Development
Federal Council for Science and Technology
Indian Arts and Crafts Board
Marine Mammal Commission
Migratory Bird Conservation Commission

Mississippi River Commission
National Advisory Committee on Occupational Safety and Health
National Advisory Council on Adult Education
National Advisory Council on the Education of Disadvantaged
   Children
National Advisory Council on Extension and Continuing Education
National Advisory Council on Vocational Education
National Archives Trust Fund Board
National Commission on Libraries and Information Science
National Commission on Water Quality
National Forest Reservation Commission
National Historical Publications and Records Commission
National Park Foundation
National Review Board for the Center for Cultural and Technical
   Interchange between East and West
Office of Science and Technology Policy
President's Commission on White House Fellowships
President's Committee on Employment of the Handicapped
President's Committee on Mental Retardation
President's Council on Physical Fitness and Sports
Regional Action Planning Commission
Susquehanna River Basin Commission
United States Advisory Commission on Information
United States Advisory Commission on International Educational
   and Cultural Affairs
Water Resources Council

Still other funding sources are the quasi-governmental agencies described in the following section.

Quasi-Governmental Agencies

This section describes a certain type of funding agency that receives its money from Congress, yet is independently advised by private citizens. These are called quasi-governmental agencies, the two major ones being:

National Foundation on the Arts and the Humanities
National Science Foundation

The first, the National Foundation on the Arts and the Humanities, is subdivided into three components:

Federal Council of the Arts and Humanities
National Endowment for the Arts
National Endowment for the Humanities

Federal Council of the Arts and Humanities

From a grant-seeker's standpoint, this subdivision will not affect you, at least not directly. Nevertheless, you should be generally aware of the Federal Council's existence and its prime function: to help coordinate the programs and activities of the two Endowments (Arts and Humanities) with those of the various federal agencies. Council membership consists of the two Endowment chairmen, one congressman, one senator, and twelve federal-agency heads.

National Endowment for the Arts (NEA)

NEA's goal is to foster American art by increasing the American public's appreciation and awareness of art, by making art more widely available, by preserving the country's cultural heritage, by encouraging and aiding the development of highly talented artists, and by helping sustain worthy, financially undernourished cultural organizations.

In achieving its goals, NEA annually dispenses about $80 million worth of competitive grants in a wide range of art-program areas, including:

> architecture and environmental arts
> crafts
> dance
> education
> expansion arts
> folk arts
> literature
> media arts
> museums
> music
> theater
> visual arts

Eligible grant recipients are individuals and tax-exempt nonprofit organizations. Projects must have a proven need for funds, must be nonprofit-making, and must hold great promise for a meaningful contribution to the art world. Moreover, the money cannot be used for deficit funding or for the purchase of fixed assets, including construction, capital improvements, equipment, and property. If you are applying as an individual, you must have previously demonstrated your exceptional talent (NEA's primary mission is not to discover new talent, but to develop it). Another virtually essential requirement is that one be a citizen or a U.S. resident foreigner. Being young and/or female sometimes works to your advantage.

The type of recipient of the individual fellowship varies widely: art critic, choreographer, composer, craftsman, creative writer, designer, film maker, jazz/folk ethnic musician, librettist, museum professional, opera singer, photographer, and print-maker. Organization recipients range from large symphony orchestras, museums, and opera and dance companies, to neigh-borhood street-theater groups, jazz clubs, and pottery work-shops.

Grant size also varies widely: from a few hundred dollars to a million dollars, generally for one-year periods. For organiza-tions (but seldom for individuals) a "matching grant" is the usual funding mechanism. These are grants that require the re-cipient to match the funds with nonfederal money on at least a dollar-for-dollar basis. A special type of matching block grant is made to the various official state art agencies for redistribu-tion to individuals and organizations within their respective states.

The NEA application steps are as follows: First, write to NEA for its free *Guide to Programs* publication. (If you already know the specific program area that relates to your project, then save time by requesting the specific *Guidelines* for that area rather than initially asking for the *Guide to Programs*.) Once you have pinpointed the program area(s) relative to your needs, write the appropriate staff program director for application forms and guidelines. If, after reviewing the information, you still think your project qualifies, then informally submit a preliminary description of your project to the appropriate staff program di-rector to ascertain your chances. If the program director gives you a green light (or suggests constructive changes), complete and send in your formal application to NEA's Grant's Office. (You can submit it even if you're given a red light, but the odds are overwhelming that you'll be wasting your time, because the staff program director is in an excellent position to assess your chances of success.) Your formal proposal is then turned over to an outside panel of consulting experts for review. Next, the panel's and the staff program director's recommendations are presented, along with your application, to the National Council on the Arts for its review and recommendations, which are then sent to the chairman of the National Endowment for the Arts. Finally, the chairman makes the ultimate go or no-go decision and notifies you by letter. The entire process takes six to nine months.

In certain cases, the chairman may speed up the application process by bypassing the normal National Council on the Arts approval step if the grant does not exceed $10,000. This is called a "Chairman's Grant."

Administratively, the NEA is run by a presidentially appointed chairman. Advising the chairman on policy, programs, and grant applications is the National Council on the Arts, whose twenty-six eminent members from the art field are also appointed by the President.

The indispensable NEA publication is its *Guide to Programs,* which succinctly describes its policies, grants, and program details, including eligibility requirements, funding amounts, and deadlines. Also worth requesting is NEA's *Cultural Post,* giving updated policy and program information (it is published every two months). Both publications are available free by writing to the address given below.

For specific details or general information, contact the appropriate NEA office, or:

> The Office of the Chairman
> National Endowment for the Arts
> 2401 E Street, N.W.
> Washington, D.C. 20506
> (202) 634–6369

National Endowment for the Humanities (NEH)

NEH's goal is to encourage and develop the study, understanding, and appreciation of humanistic knowledge as it relates to individuals and to national concerns.

Some $80 million is annually awarded to grant-seekers in a broad spectrum of humanistic study areas such as:

> archaeology
> comparative religion
> ethics
> history
> history and criticism of the arts
> jurisprudence
> linguistics
> literature
> modern and classical language
> philosophy

Another study area that is fundable encompasses those facets of the social-science disciplines (cultural anthropology, international relations, political theory, sociology, et cetera) that relate historically or philosophically to the humanities.

Eligible grant recipients are individuals and nonprofit organizations pursuing projects relating to NEH's goals. Individual applicants—in almost every case—must be citizens or, if foreign nationals, must have resided in the United States for at least three years. Typical organization recipients include colleges, community groups, historical and other cultural societies, libraries, public agencies, radio and TV stations, cable television access centers, and secondary and elementary schools.

Among the project costs seldom funded are work leading toward an academic degree, construction and restoration, procurement of permanent equipment, museum and library acquisitions. The same nonfunding restrictions apply to training, performance, or creative work in the arts, as those areas of endeavor fall under the jurisdiction of the NEA.

As with its sister agency NEA, NEH is administered by its own chairman, presidentially appointed. Similarly, NEH has its own separate budget as well as an advisory board—in this case, the National Council on the Humanities—composed of twenty-six distinguished citizens from the humanities field. NEH's application process is also very much like that employed by NEA.

NEH administers its funding programs through these sub-units:

Division of Education: Mostly supports programs that improve the formalized teaching of the humanities. Chief recipients: educational institutions.

Division of Fellowships: Awards stipends and fellowships to scholars, teachers, nonacademic humanists, and various professionals embarking on independent study or research projects.

Division of Public Programs: Funds programs that increase the availability of the humanities to the adult, nonstudent public. Chief recipients are media organizations, museums and historic societies.

Office of State Board Programs: Redistributes funds on a state and local level.

Division of Research Grants: Supports long-term group (as opposed to individual) research programs, including text editing and the operation of research collections.

Office of Planning and Analysis: Administers the "Youthgrants in the Humanities Program." Chief recipients: students and other young people.

Challenge Grants: Supports basic operating expenses of humanities institutions by matching one federal dollar for every three dollars raised privately.

Grants to individuals are almost always of the nonmatching kind, while those awarded to organizations may require some form of cost-sharing or matching funds from a nonfederal source.

NEH's principal publication for grant-seekers is its *Program Announcement* guide, a booklet summarizing its funding program policies, application procedures, deadlines, and other pertinent information. In addition, each NEH division publishes its own specialized guide booklet. Another useful publication is NEH's *Annual Report,* which reviews previously funded programs, thereby giving you added insight into NEH's funding patterns. NEH's *Humanities* newsletter also gives grant reports. All three publications are available free from the address given below.

For specific details or general information, contact the appropriate NEH office, or:

> Office of the Chairman
> National Endowment for the Humanities
> 806 15th Street, N.W.
> Washington, D.C. 20506
> (202) 382–7465

National Science Foundation (NSF)

NSF's master objective is to strengthen the country's scientific capability. NSF fulfills its congressionally mandated mission by awarding grants to:

Programs that increase the country's scientific knowledge and programs that increase the country's scientific research capabilities.
Programs that facilitate scientific information exchange, both domestically and internationally.
Programs that improve the quality of scientific education.
Programs that help train scientists.
Programs that accelerate the nation's implementation of R&D breakthroughs.

Principal NSF grant recipients are academic institutions and nonprofit research institutions. A commercial organization, however, can also receive a grant if it offers an otherwise unavailable product or service that is necessary for reaching an NSF goal.

NSF's $800 million annual budget flows into a wide delta of scientific fields, including the anthropological, astronomical, biochemical, biological, chemical, computer, energy, engineering, environmental, geological, mathematical, medical, oceanic, physical, and social sciences. Areas not funded include clinical medicine, business, social work, and the arts and humanities.

To give you a clearer idea of the specific types of programs NSF funds, here is a representative sampling: Arctic Research, Graduate Fellowships, International Travel Grants, Minority Institutions Science Improvement, Ocean Sediment Coring, Public Understanding of Science, Research Applied to Natural Needs (RANN), United States-India Exchange of Scientists, and Women in Science.

Grant size can range anywhere from a thousand to a million or more dollars. Grant periods are usually for a duration of one year or less. However, multiyear grant periods are not uncommon (unlike NEA and NEH grants).

Administratively, NSF is run by a presidentially appointed director. The governing body is the National Science Board, consisting of the NSF director and twenty-four distinguished representatives from the science community. Under the director are these six operating directorates:

> Astronomical, Atmospheric,
>   Earth and Ocean Sciences
> Biological, Behavioral and Social Sciences
> Mathematical and Physical
>   Sciences and Engineering
> Research Applications
> Science Education
> Scientific Technological,
>   and International Affairs

These directorates are further broken down into divisions and sections, each responsible for the basic review and administration of the grants falling into their respective areas.

Here is a brief run-down of the NSF application procedure. First, request and read the NSF *Guide to Programs.* This booklet will help you determine which (if any) of the NSF programs are realistic funding sources for your project. Next, write the appropriate NSF division or section officer for application forms and guidelines. After studying them, submit an informal description of your project to the appropriate NSF staff officer. This officer can usually give you a quick answer on whether it would be worth your time to pursue your NSF grant quest. Sometimes he will suggest project alterations that will improve its fundability at NSF. Your next step is to submit the final application to the Central Processing Section in care of the specific program. Your application will then be reviewed by the staff officer and outside experts. Their recommendations, along with your application, are passed along to the National Science Board, which makes the final decision. Between the time you make your first inquiry and the day the decision arrives in the mail, six to nine months will probably have elapsed.

NSF deserves praise for the useful publications it makes available to grant-seekers. Its basic publication is the previously mentioned *Guide to Programs,* a booklet briefly describing NSF's programs and the program specifics such as eligibility requirements and deadlines. Another highly instructional NSF booklet is *Grants for Scientific Research.* Though prepared for scientific-research grant-seekers, it is so filled with general "how to apply for a government grant" information that it is a must for anyone seeking not only an NSF grant, but government grants in general. Still other NSF publications worth obtaining include the ten-times-a-year *Bulletin* newsletter giving current program information, including deadlines, and the *Organizational Directory* listing the telephone and room numbers of program staff members. All these publications, plus specialized proposal preparation guidelines for most of the NSF program areas, are available free by writing to the address given below. For $8.55, you can receive a subscription to the quarterly *Mosaic,* the official NSF magazine containing well-written background articles on the agency's activities and plans. A good outside source of NSF program announcements and changes is Commerce Business Daily (see page 161).

For specific details or general information, contact the appropriate NSF office, or:

> Office of the Director
> National Science Foundation
> 1800 G Street, N.W.
> Washington, D.C. 20550
> (202) 655-4000

The Quasi-Official Governmental Agencies

There are a number of independent agencies that receive funds from the Federal government in return for advisory and other services. These bodies include:

> Institute of Medicine
> National Academy of Engineering
> National Academy of Sciences
> National Research Council

All four of these quasi-official governmental agencies are excellent background sources of specialized information for government grant- and contract-seekers because they are deeply involved in helping the government formulate its grant and contract policies. All four agencies share the same address and telephone number:

> 2101 Constitution Avenue, N.W.
> Washington, D.C. 20418
> (202) 393-8100

State and Local Governmental Agencies

Consistent with the New Federalism philosophy, more and more grants are being awarded by state and local governments. Though the aggregate dollar total of these grants is small in comparison to the grant money dispensed by the Federal government, these state and local government granting programs are still significantly large.

The funds used to underwrite these grant programs are chiefly self-generated through state and local tax programs. However, an increasing amount of the needed dollars is coming to the state and local governments from the Federal government through such funding mechanisms as Community Block Grants (see page 84), the Comprehensive Employment Training Act (see page 87), and General Revenue Sharing (see page 95). Collectively, the various federal-to-state and federal-to-local government funding mechanisms distribute an estimated $60 billion a year.

As these decentralized funding programs continue to increase, it becomes even more important to know how to deal with the state and local grant-making agencies. In general, the process of applying for state and local grants is more or less the same as for federal grants. Specifically, there are critical differences worth noting:

Competition: In most instances the competition for state and local funding dollars is keener than for federal dollars.

Regulations: With literally thousands of different governmental state and local granting agencies, each with its own independent governing body, you will be encountering a wide variety of funding regulations. Sometimes a program will even require you to meet simultaneously three (sometimes contradictory) levels of regulations: federal, state, and local. Despite these headaches, there is no getting around the fact that you must understand the regulations of your state and local governments as thoroughly as possible if you want to compete successfully for their funds.

Grant-Dollar Availability: Even on a per capita basis, local governments (and to some degree, state governments) differ in the amount and type of funds they have available to give to grant-seekers. To illustrate, let's take two hypothetical hundred-thousand-population cities, "A" and "B." City A may be more aggressive and thorough than city B in getting flow-through money from its state and Federal governments and hence may have more money to distribute to its local grant-seekers. Or city A may give a large share of its General Revenue Sharing funds to its grant-seeking community service organizations while city B may use the GRS money to help support its police and fire departments.

Method of Payment: While Federal government grantees are almost always given their funds in advance, most state and local government grantees, however, receive their funds only after they submit an expense report. This procedure can create a cash-flow problem, especially to organizations and individuals suffering from a shortage of working capital.

Conventional Approach: The smaller the granting governmental unit, the more it tends to fund conventional as opposed to innovative projects.

Politics: State and especially locally administered grant programs are more susceptible to being politically influenced than those run by the Federal government. For example, many a local project has been selected over a more worthy competitor because it was capable of gaining the most favorable media coverage for the local politicians. Another somewhat common occurrence is political favoritism: perhaps the grant-seeking executive helped elect a politician through volunteer or monetary contributions. But, to put these phenomena in proper perspective, at least 95 percent of state and 90 percent of local grants are awarded objectively and without bias.

Information Availability: Except in a few states such as California, Virginia, and Florida, state-level grant program information is seriously inadequate. Even for the three states mentioned, the quality and quantity of the information is a far cry from that disseminated by the Federal government. On a local level, the availability of grant program information is even worse.

The best source of information on a state or local government funding program is obviously the funding agency itself. For example, the various quasi-governmental State Councils of the Arts provide you with data such as their eligibility requirements and application procedures. This type of specific information is usually unobtainable from outside sources.

If you are unaware of all the state-level grant programs that relate to your project, your best initial step is to contact your governor's office. Its staff should be able either to supply you with the needed data or to direct you to the appropriate official or published material. On a local level, the best initial source is usually the office of the chief executive (mayor, county supervisor, et cetera). Your state or local government's budgetary office is also a useful data source, as are your funding competitors.

The Federal government publishes some useful information too. Data in the *Catalog of Federal Domestic Assistance* (see page 124) sometimes identifies the state agency responsible for granting federal flow-through funds. For general background statistical data on federal assistance to state and local governments, write:

Office of Management and Budget
Executive Office Building
Washington, D.C. 20503

and ask for a free copy of its *Special Analysis O*. Also write:

Treasury Department
15th Street and Pennsylvania Avenue N.W.
Washington, D.C. 20220

for its free booklet, *Federal Aid to States,* which breaks down the aid by federal agency, then by major program. An even more detailed state-by-state funding breakdown is published in a series of regional budget books compiled by the Federal Regional Council. Sometimes your own Regional Council (see page 145) will have extra copies.

PART THREE
Information
Sources

INTRODUCTION TO
PART THREE

Part Three, we believe, is the most comprehensive directory of major government-grant information sources ever compiled. It is the result of a massive search that uncovered numerous publications and services, both useful and useless. None of the latter is listed in our book. Neither have we attempted to itemize all the thousands upon thousands of specialized sources that focus on particular fields. There are simply too many of these to include within a single volume (but we do give you a few pointers on how to discover their existence yourself).

Part Three is arranged as follows. The first section gives general tips on obtaining grant information. The next five sections describe six major official Federal government information sources:

> Catalog of Federal Domestic Assistance
> Federal Register
> Federal Information Centers
> Federal Regional Councils
> Federal Circulars
> Federal Assistance Programs Retrieval System

The final section, "Other Sources of Information," describes sixty additional key information sources, governmental and private.

GENERAL TIPS ON
Obtaining
Information

Freedom of Information Act

Every grant-seeker should be familiar with the Freedom of Information Act. It requires (with certain exceptions) that the Executive Branch provide you with the following information upon request: agency rules, policy statements, reports, records, proceedings, and administrative staff manuals, among other data.

The key exceptions are information pertaining to national security, to internal personnel records and practices, to intra-governmental memos, to specific statutory exceptions such as income tax returns, to trade secrets, and to confidential data relating to banks, oil-well maps, and certain other sensitive commercial information areas.

Your right of access to Executive Branch information is guaranteed by the 1966 Federal Information Act—and by its 1974 amendments, which stipulate that the agencies must furnish the data free or at cost and within a reasonable amount of time.

The Freedom of Information Act in its entirety is printed in the *U.S. Government Manual* (see page 187). You can also obtain a free copy of the act (see "Copies of Congressional Bills" section, page 165). Virtually all agencies have issued their own specific regulations concerning the act, which are available free by writing to the appropriate agency.

Government Printing Office

GPO prints and distributes over twenty-five thousand different publications that are prepared, for the most part, by the various federal agencies. These publications vary in size from small pamphlets, to monthly periodicals, to massive hard-cover volumes. Prices range from free to over $100 (for a first-class-mail annual subscription to *Commerce Business Daily*).

The principal directories of the available GPO publications are the *GPO Monthly Catalog* (see page 175), the *GPO Selected U.S. Government Publications booklet* (see page 176), and the various *GPO Individual Select Bibliographies* lists (see page 175).

Here are some of the ground rules when ordering from the GPO:

Give exact title (GPO also suggests that you give the publication number, though this is not mandatory).

Full advance payment is required. Send check or money order—never cash or stamps.

You can order more than one publication or subscription with a single payment. However, to speed up the fulfillment process, GPO requests that you put each order on a separate piece of paper, along with your name and address.

You are given a 25 percent discount on orders of one hundred copies or more of a single title mailed to the same address.

If your requested publication is temporarily out of print, your order is automatically back-ordered and will be fulfilled when new copies come off the press. If the publication is permanently out of print, your payment will be refunded.

Once your order has been processed, GPO starts your subscription with the next issue published. You cannot request that your subscription start with the issue date of your choosing.

GPO will not back-issue your subscription. If you want back issues, order them separately at the individual-copy rate.

For a subscription order, plan to wait about three months before

you receive the first issue. For a nonsubscription order, such as a booklet, the waiting period averages six weeks to three months.
For subscription renewals, you will automatically receive a GPO computerized renewal card about three months prior to expiration of your current subscription. If by chance you don't receive one, renew as soon as possible by sending in the appropriate payment and the mailing label from one of your recent issues.

All GPO publications may be ordered from

> Superintendent of Documents
> U.S. Government Printing Office
> Washington, D.C. 20402.

In addition, a limited selection of publications is sold in the GPO Bookstores (see page 174).

Reference copies of many GPO publications are available for perusal at Depository Libraries (see page 166).

Some Additional Tips on Government Sources

Some GPO-sold publications can be obtained free—and usually much more quickly—if you request them from the federal agency that originated the document. However, there are two potential drawbacks to this method. Drawback number 1 is that you can request only a single copy. The second drawback occurs when the agency does not have free copies available, either because it has run out of them or because it was never issued to them by the GPO in the first place. In such instances the agency will simply refer you to the GPO, thereby adding a further time delay to the already slow GPO ordering process. What, then, is the best source, the agency or the GPO? On balance, ordering directly from the agency is usually the best approach because of the speed factor. To insure yourself against the possibility that your agency request will be returned unfulfilled, submit a simultaneous order to the GPO.

If your original request for information goes unanswered, by all means try again. But this time be sure to mention the fact that your first request was not fulfilled. Saying so often brings a prompt reply because of the agency official's fear of violating the Freedom of Information Act.

Try to get on every applicable mailing list—for newsletters, bulletins, press releases, what have you. They provide good background information and sometimes serve as early warning systems to program changes. If an agency turns down your request, ask why. More often than not the agency will put you on its mailing list rather than risk a potential dispute.

To whom should you mail a request? If you are unsure of the proper office or official, it's almost always better to direct your request to the higher level and let it drift downward.

When requesting information from a government agency, you might consider using this field-tested form letter, or a suitable adaptation. It's simple, brief, direct—and it works:

Dear (Mr. Doe):
Please rush me a copy of _____.
Please also send me any other material relating to the following subject area: _____.
In addition, please put me on your mailing list for any periodical or future publication that may relate to that subject area.
Thank you for your kind assistance.
Sincerely,

Always be as specific as possible in describing the information you desire. Chances are you will receive the information with greater speed and certainty if you ask for "information on your XYZ Drug Abuse program (number 000-000-0000)" rather than requesting "information on your drug-abuse program." Reason: sometimes the government official may be working on two related drug-abuse programs and consequently confusion may result on your request.

Some Pointers on Private Information Sources

A number of private grant-information publishing and/or consulting firms are described later in our "Other Sources of Information" section. Their fees, specialties, and scope of services vary; and some are nonprofit organizations while others are money-making enterprises. It is almost impossible to gather them under one descriptive umbrella.

The principal users of these services tend to be medium-sized organizations. While most of the information these services publish is readily available directly from the government, the users often lack either the time, staff, expertise, contacts, or desire to do the bothersome research chores themselves. In short, they believe it is more efficient to pay an outside specialist to do the work.

Well-staffed large organizations, on the other hand, usually assign most of the research chores to in-house personnel.

Small grant-seeking organizations and individuals seldom purchase the outside services—especially the several-hundred-dollar-a-year variety—because of limited budgets.

Are these services worth the money they charge? Invariably the answer is yes or no, depending principally on two factors. The first is the grant-seeker's individual needs. All services listed in this book are of value to at least some, but not all, grant-seekers. This phenomenon is logical because, with the complexity of the government-grant field, no one service can be all things to all clients. The second factor is how well you use the services once you receive them. Our experience has shown that too many grant-seekers ineffectually use the excellent information inputs they pay for.

Only you are in a position to determine accurately which outside services (if any) suit your needs and purse. But since these services are usually on the costly side, it makes sense to investigate and cross-compare their individual merits before financially committing yourself. Make a list of the most promising prospects, then write them for descriptive literature and, if applicable, for sample copies of their periodicals. Remember, most newsletters and magazines—especially the quality ones described in this book—are more than happy to oblige you. After all, they have (or should have) so much confidence in the usefulness of their published material that they believe you'll want to subscribe once you've had an opportunity to review a sample issue. If a periodical (or service) proves to be not worth the price, you've lost only a postage stamp plus some secretarial and reading time. On the other hand, if it proves useful, you may ultimately gain a great deal of incremental funds.

Catalog of Federal Domestic Assistance

The *Catalog* is easily the single most valuable source of information in the government grant-seeking field. It is an official U.S. Government publication.

Essentially, the *Catalog* is a massive work of nearly a thousand loose-leaf pages that lists and describes practically all federal programs and activities that socially or economically aid the public. Its chief function is to help grant-seekers identify and obtain information on the types and sources of available federal assistance.

Covered in the *Catalog* are over a thousand domestic-aid programs sponsored by some fifty federal departments, independent agencies, commissions, and councils. These programs range alphabetically from "academic computing services" to "zoo display animals, disposal of surplus wildlife," and encompass many form of aid including grants, loans and loan guarantees, scholarships, training, technical assistance, statistical data, equipment and facilities.

The *Catalog* is divided into four basic sections: Indexes, Program Changes, Program Descriptions, and Appendixes, in that order.

Indexes

The indexes are worth mastering, as they are significant timesavers. Without them, the identification of relevant programs in the *Catalog* would be a formidable task.

There are eight quick-reference indexes, each serving a different purpose:

Agency Program Index: This index (see sample below) is useful in determining which programs a particular federal agency sponsors. Each individual program is categorized according to the sponsoring agency, then subcategorized according to the specific subdivision within the agency. Each program is further codified by the program number, such as 10.001. (Program numbers will be described in more detail later.) These programs are arranged in numerical sequence in the *Catalog's* "Program Description" section. Each program is also codified by a letter such as A, B, or C. This letter indicates the type of assistance offered by the program. (The *Catalog* deciphers these letters for you in the front part of the book.) Here is an extract:

DEPARTMENT OF AGRICULTURE

AGRICULTURAL RESEARCH SERVICE

10.001   Agricultural Research—Basic and Applied Research (B,L)

ANIMAL AND PLANT HEALTH INSPECTION SERVICE

10.025   Plant and Animal Disease and Pest Control (J,I.)
10.026   Assistance to States for Intrastate Meat and Poultry Inspection (B)
10.027   Meat and Poultry Inspection (J)

AGRICULTURAL STABILIZATION AND CONSERVATION SERVICE

10.051   Commodity Loans and Purchases (D,E)
10.052   Cotton Production Stabilization (D)
10.053   Dairy Indemnity Payments (D)
10.054   Emergency Conservation Measures (B)

Applicant Eligibility Index—Individual: This identifies programs for which individuals are eligible. As with the next three indexes we'll be describing, the programs in this index are classified into eighteen broad categories such as "Education," "Housing," and "Natural Resources." These categories are further broken down into a combined total of approximately one hundred subcategories. For instance, under "Education" come "Facilities and Equipment," "General Research," and other subcategories. Here is an extract:

EDUCATION

FACILITIES AND EQUIPMENT
13.676   Surplus Property Utilization (H)
15.109   Indian Education—Dormitory Operations (J)

GENERAL RESEARCH

13.565   Women's Educational Equity (B,P)
13.950   Educational Research and Development (B,P)
17.233   Employment and Training Research and Development Projects (B)
24.035   Research and Development in Energy Conservation (B)

Applicant Eligibility Index Local [Government]: This identifies programs for which local governments are eligible.

Applicant Eligibility Index Nonprofit Organizations and Institutions: This lists programs for which nonprofit organizations and institutions may make application.

Applicant Eligibility Index State [Government]: This identifies programs for which state governments are eligible.

Functional Index: This index pigeonholes all programs in broad functional categories. These categories are identical to the ones used in the three Eligibility Indexes.

Popular Name Index: Some of the programs have both an official and informal name. The "Veterans Educational Assistance" program is a case in point, as it is frequently referred to in the press as the "GI Bill." Thus, the need for this index. Listings are alphabetical.

Subject Index: Programs are classified under key words or phrases such as "Allergy, research." This is the best of the seven indexes to use if you are "fishing" for a program matching your interests—but bear in mind that this index has not been exhaustively compiled and, therefore, has some omissions. Here is a sample extract:

> Allergy, research, 13.855
> Allied health professions developmental grants, 13.305
> American flag vessels, operating subsidies, *see* Sea transportation
> Animals, damage control, 15.601
> Animals, diseases, *see* Laboratory animals; Veterinary medicine
> Annual allotment program, 15.951
> Anthropology, *see* Social sciences
> Antidumping duties, 21.200
> Antipoverty programs
>   Community Action, 49.002
>   Community Economic Development, 49.011
>   minigrants to public and private organizations, 72.010
>   Older Persons Opportunities and Services, 49.010
>   State Economic and Opportunity Offices, 49.013
> AOP, 17.200

Program Changes

The primary purpose of this short section is to alert readers of last year's *Catalog* to any program that has been deleted from or added to the new edition. Programs that have undergone name or number changes are also noted.

Program Descriptions

The core of the *Catalog* is the "Program Description" section, comprising over 80 percent of the total pages. Its primary purpose is to give you some of the specific details of a program once you have located it through the indexes.

Information for all programs is presented in a standardized format. To acquaint you with this format, we have reprinted below an actual sample. While the specifics vary from program to program, the bold-face headings remain the same. The circled numbers are ours and correspond to our explanatory comments that follow the sample entry.

60.013 SMITHSONIAN INSTITUTION
TRAVELING EXHIBITION SERVICE
(SITES)

FEDERAL AGENCY: SMITHSONIAN INSTITUTION

AUTHORIZATION: Act of Congress approved August 10, 1846; 20 U.S.C. 41 et seq.

OBJECTIVES: To provide a public service by the circulation of exhibitions on a wide range of subjects throughout the United States and Canada.

TYPES OF ASSISTANCE: Use of Property, Facilities, and Equipment; Provision of Specialized Services.

USES AND USE RESTRICTIONS: A broad range of exhibitions available to museums of all sizes and character, art galleries, and educational organizations and institutions. Exhibitions of both flat and 3D materials. Occasional supplementary lectures and films. May be used for educational purposes only. No special admission may be charged by borrowing organization without prior approval by the Smithsonian Institution Traveling Exhibition Service.

ELIGIBILITY REQUIREMENTS:
  Applicant Eligibility: Individuals or groups.
  Beneficiary Eligibility: Same as applicant eligibility.
  Credentials/Documentation: Borrowers must satisfy requirements of appropriate space, lighting, heating, air conditioning, police and fire protection, and handling of exhibitions to qualify as a borrower from the Smithsonian Traveling Exhibition Service.

APPLICATION AND AWARD PROCESS:
  Preapplication Coordination: None.
  Application Procedure: Written. A signed contract is required of the exhibitor before each booking. Forms and details furnished upon request.
  Aware Procedure: Not applicable.
  Deadlines: Most available immediately.
  Range of Approval/Disapproval Time: Varies according to exhibition and requesters' requirements.
  Appeals: Not applicable.
  Renewals: Exhibitions are offered for 4-week periods unless otherwise specified. Upon request extended or double bookings can be arranged.

ASSISTANCE CONSIDERATIONS:
  Formula and Matching Requirements: The borrower pays rental, protection, and outgoing transportation costs.
  Length and Time Phasing of Assistance: See Renewals above.

POST ASSISTANCE REQUIREMENTS:
  Reports: Publicity: The borrower agrees to give credit to SITES, as well as to designated lenders, organizers, and/or sponsors of the exhibition, in all acknowledgements, press releases, and catalogs. The borrower agrees to

send SITES copies of all press clippings for forwarding to the lenders. Borrower agrees to furnish condition reports on receipt of exhibition and further agrees to wire or phone SITES in case of any change (damage, theft, etc.) during exhibition period.

Audits: As called for in contract.

Records: As called for in contract.

FINANCIAL INFORMATION:

Account Identification: 32-50-0100-0-1-503.

Obligations: (Salaries and expenses) FY 75 $105,000; FY 76 est $99,000; TQ est $25,000; and FY 77 est $102,000.

Range and Average of Financial Assistance: Not applicable.

PROGRAM ACCOMPLISHMENTS: During fiscal year 1975, from 100 to 120 individual exhibitions circulated throughout the United States and Canada, moving about 6 times per year, or 720 showings per year reviewed by millions of people.

REGULATIONS, GUIDELINES, AND LITERATURE: Exhibitions listing issued. Individual exhibition catalogs. "Smithsonian Year."

INFORMATION CONTACTS:

Regional or Local Office: None.

Headquarters Office: Director, Smithsonian Institution Traveling Exhibition Service, Office of Museum Programs, Smithsonian Institution, Washington, DC 20560 Telephone (202) 381-6631.

RELATED PROGRAMS: 45.007. Promotion of the Arts State and Community Operations, 60.001. Smithsonian Institution Programs in Basic Research and Public Education; 68.001. National Gallery of Art Extension Service.

Here is what you should know—including some special tips —on each bold-face heading:

1 *Program Number:* Each program is assigned a five-digit number such as 60.013 (as in our sample). The first two digits indicate the sponsoring agency (60 specifies the Smithsonian Institution). The digits to the right of the decimal point (.013 in our sample) identify the appropriate subdivision of the agency. This five-digit number is important, as it must be included in a grant application.

2 *Program Title:* The agencies try to make this title as descriptive as possible.

3 *Popular Name:* The acronym, abbreviation, or nickname of the official title. Usually this is the name most people use in day-to-day conversation.

4 *Federal Agency:* Specifies the name of the administering agency and subdivision, if applicable. However, for the specific office, you must refer to "Information Contacts" (see Number 16).

5 *Authorization:* Tells you which specific legislation authorized the program. This allows you to obtain a copy of the law (from your congressman, the GPO, et cetera) and read it with a fine-toothed comb. Another benefit—and this is an important one—is that you can quote segments of the legislation in your proposal, thereby strengthening it in the eyes of most government-proposal reviewers. You are also given the date or dates a law was enacted, a fact often critical to you because many laws are changed after their initial passage. Therefore the more recent the date, the less the chance that the program will have been altered. In assessing the date, you must take into consideration the type of program, as some types of legislation are dynamic (poverty programs, for example are often in a constant state of flux), while others remain static, as is the case with our Smithsonian Institution sample, which was originally put into law in 1846.

6 *Objectives:* By succinctly stating the purpose of the program, this piece of information helps you to determine quickly whether there is enough of a match-up between your needs and the program's goal to warrant your spending more time reading the rest of the program description. Number 8, the *"Uses and Use Restrictions"* part of the Program Description, further helps you clarify the objective.

7 *Types of Assistance:* Tells you which kind of aid is being offered. The sixteen types of aid are defined in the *Catalog*'s introduction.

8 *Uses and Use Restrictions:* Specifies how the funds may or may not be used.

9 *Eligibility Requirements:* States who may apply for and administer the funds as well as who may receive the benefits of the program. The required credentials and proof of credentials of the grant-seekers are also specified.

10 *Application and Award Process:* Presents a number of essential details. The first, "Preapplication Coordination" specifies a number of critical requirements such as when the A-95 Clearinghouse review process is applicable and whether the procedures in a particular Federal Management Circular (such as FMC 74–7) must be followed. Item 10 also helps you work out a realistic time plan by giving you deadline dates for submission and the expected length of time required by the agency to make a go or no-go decision. Procedures for appeals and renewals are also indicated.

11 *Assistance Considerations:* The first part stipulates whether a portion of the budget must be absorbed by another funding source or by your organization. The second part indicates the duration and method of payment of the grant award.

12 *Post Assistance Requirements:* Establishes which reports are required, which accounting procedures must be followed, and the types of audits you can expect.

13 *Financial Information:* Keep in mind that the *Catalog*'s figures are estimates at best. What you need to find out is how many dollars are still available. (A letter or call to the office listed in Item 16, "Information Contacts," should supply you with an updated answer.)

14 *Program Accomplishments:* This item, by showing you a funding agency's track record, will give you additional information on what the funding agency really wants to do with its dollars.

15 *Regulations, Guidelines and Literature:* Tells you of available printed information relating to the program. Most can be ordered by writing directly to the agency. Reviewing this material provides you with a competitive edge and can sometimes mean the difference between succeeding and failing in your grant pursuit.

16 *Information Contacts:* The "Headquarters Office" entry gives you the title of the official administering the program. If you are also given the name of a regional or local office, all the better, because this office (and its official) is a decentralized source of useful data and—quite possibly—has direct or indirect decision-making authority.

17 *Related Programs:* A rough guide to other programs in the *Catalog* that may also serve your needs.

Appendixes

The *Catalog* has a number of very useful appendixes that give you:

A columnar guide, telling you at a glance whether a particular program requires the A-95, FMC 74-4, FMC 74-7, Environmental Impact Statement or TC 1082 process,

A cross-indexed list of the congressional acts and executive orders that mandate the programs in the *Catalog*,

A directory of frequently used abbreviations and acronyms,
A detailed directory of the names, addresses, and telephone numbers
of the various regional and local offices of U.S. Government
agencies,
A nationwide directory of Federal Information Centers, Federal
Regional Councils, and Federal Executive Boards,
Deadlines for applications submitted.

The Supplement

In the back of the *Catalog* is a postcard. Return it and you'll
receive free the *Catalog's* Supplement, which is published and
mailed to you sometime in midwinter.

This annual update lists programs that have been added,
deleted, or modified since the publication of the *Catalog*. Also
included are full descriptions of new programs and complete
revised sets of the indexes and appendixes.

There are two basic ways to deal with the Supplement when
it arrives. If you use the *Catalog* frequently and have the extra
staff power, replace all the appropriate pages, one by one. If
this is not practical (as is the case with most fund-seekers), then
replace the indexes and appendixes, go over the list of program
changes, replace and/or annotate the programs you know will
directly affect you, and—finally—insert the remainder of the
material at the front of your loose-leaf binder for possible future
reference.

If you order the *Catalog* after the Supplement is published,
you will receive the *Catalog* and Supplement simultaneously,
though not conveniently combined. You will still have the chore
of removing the out-of-date pages and adding the appropriate
updated ones.

How to Order

The *Catalog of Federal Domestic Assistance* generally comes
off the press in early summer and can be ordered for $16 from:

> Superintendent of Documents
> U.S. Government Printing Office
> Washington, D.C. 20402

A price increase is expected. And, the *Catalog* no longer comes with a large three-ring binder, but you can find a suitable substitute at your local stationery store.

A word of warning: Because of the inefficiency in processing your order, it can take two months or more between the time you place your order and the day the *Catalog* arrives in the mail, even if you ordered it months before publication date, so order as far in advance as possible. Or, if you have a contact in the nation's capital, have him purchase a copy for you at the main GPO bookstore in Washington, D.C. (Sadly, the Federal Bookstores around the country do not currently stock the *Catalog*.)

If you use and have access to data-processing equipment, you might investigate the possibility of purchasing select elements of the *Catalog* on computer tape. For the details, write:

> National Technical Information Service
> U.S. Department of Commerce
> Springfield, Virginia 22151

Should your expected use of the *Catalog* not warrant the investment, you can find a reference copy at most large public and college libraries. Xerox the pertinent pages.

Limitations of the CATALOG

When using the *Catalog,* try to keep in mind its data shortcomings.

Somewhere between 10 to 20 percent of the printed information is probably out of date by the time the pages roll off the press. And some of the essential data has been intentionally or inadvertently omitted. One reason is that OMB, the compiler of the *Catalog,* is at the mercy of the funding agencies for accurate and comprehensive data—and these agencies do not always fully cooperate. Another reason for the lack of current data is that it is collected several months or more prior to publication, not to mention the inordinate delay between the publication date and the receipt of the material by you, the purchaser.

Despite these failings, the *Catalog* is indispensable for most government grant-seekers. Just imagine working without it.

Federal Register

The *Federal Register* is the most up-to-date published source of information on new and proposed agency rules and regulations, on Presidential Proclamations and Executive Orders, and on a wide variety of other Executive Branch documents of public concern. It is an official government periodical published daily, Monday through Friday.

Though only a fraction of the *Federal Register*'s content is relevant to government grant-seekers (or to contract-seekers), the relevant data is so vital that it makes the *Register* must reading, especially if your government grant-seeking operation is of sufficient size to warrant assigning someone an hour or two a day to scan the documents. (In a year's time tens of thousands of pages are published.)

The *Federal Register* is an excellent data source because almost all federal-agency funding rules and regulations must by law be published in the *Register* before programs can be funded. Moreover, the guidelines of some programs can be found only in the *Register*.

On the other hand, the *Register* is not all-inclusive. While agencies comply with the spirit of the data dissemination requirement most of the time, the announcement of the rules and regulations of some programs are tardily published or sometimes, despite the law, never published at all.

Another weakness of the *Register* is its language: a bit too lawyerish for the layman, as this typical example will show:

NATIONAL FOUNDATION ON THE ARTS AND THE HUMANITIES

ARCHITECTURE + ENVIRONMENTAL ARTS ADVISORY PANEL

Meeting

Pursuant to Section 10(a)(2) of the Federal Advisory Committee Act (Public Law 92–463), notice is hereby given that a closed meeting of the Architecture + Environmental Arts Advisory Panel to the National Endowment for the Arts will be held on July 27–28, 1976 in room 1133 of the Columbia Plaza Office Building, 2401 E Street NW., Washington, D.C. The hours will be from 9:30 a.m.–5:30 p.m. on both days.

This meeting is for the purpose of Panel review, discussion, evaluation, and recommendation on applications for financial assistance under the National Foundation on the Arts and the Humanities Act of 1965, as amended, including discussion of information given in confidence to the agency by grant applicants. In accordance with the determination of the Chairman published in the Federal Register of June 16, 1975, this meeting, which involves matters exempt from the requirements of public disclosure under the provisions of the Freedom of Information Act (5 U.S.C. 552(b), (4), (5), and (6)) will not be open to the public.

' Further information with reference to this meeting can be obtained from Mr. Robert M. Sims, Advisory Committee Management Officer, National Endowment for the Arts, Washington, D.C. 20506, or call (202) 634–6377.

ROBERT M. SIMS,
Administrative Officer, National Endowment for the Arts, National Foundation on the Arts, and the Humanities.

[FR Doc.76-19506 Filed 7–6–76;8:45 am]

A typical edition of the *Federal Register* is divided into a number of sections: Highlights, List of CFR Parts Affected, Reminders, Rules and Regulations, Proposed Rules, and Notices. In addition, there is often a Part II, Part III, and so on. Each of these sections is briefly explained below:

Highlights: An at-a-glance summary of the major documents contained in the issue. The "Highlights" section begins on the cover page and continues inside.

Contents: Documents are listed alphabetically by agency.

List of CFR Parts Affected: An index to documents that alter or may alter the regulations published in the current *Code of Federal Regulations* (CFR) publications. Both a "this issue" and a "cumulative" list are given.

Reminders: Rules that immediately go into effect and a list of public bills that have recently become law are also presented.

Rules and Regulations: Announcements of new, revised, and deleted rules and regulations that have just or are about to become official. The sample on page 136 is from this section. Data generally include eligibility requirements, application procedures, deadline dates, and other relevant information—but not the total grant dollars available. This will update your *Catalog of Federal Domestic Assistance* long before you receive the Supplement and the new annual edition. In fact, if you wait for the information to appear in the *Catalog* or in its Supplement, you will have lost a valuable head start over your competition—and you may even find out that the program's dollars or application deadline date have expired before the *Catalog* or its Supplement comes off the press. For instance, a large number of application deadline dates become effective a few months, if not a few weeks, after the official notification appears in the *Federal Register*. Obviously, information on such programs is out of date by the time the *Catalog* is published. As this evidence suggests, the *Federal Register* is an extremely valuable tool for government grant-seekers.

Proposed Rules: This section gives you a chance to voice your opinion (via letter or in person) on proposed regulations before they become official. But unless your arguments are overwhelmingly compelling, or unless you carry a big political stick, don't get your hopes up too high that you will alter the agency's preconceived course of action. The fact is that most rules and regulations are put into operation more or less as they were originally proposed in the *Federal Register*. For most grant-seekers, the significant value of this section is in alerting you to new, revised, or deleted rules and regulations before they become official—thus giving you invaluable lead time.

Notices: If a document of public interest does not conveniently fit into "Rules and Regulations" or "Proposed Rules," it is placed in this catchall. Generally, this Notice section is not as rich a source of information for grant-seekers as are the other two just mentioned, but occasionally information that may concern you does appear, such as an announcement of an important forthcoming meeting.

PART II, PART III (et cetera): These are usually self-contained mini-*Federal Registers,* each with a specific topical focus. For instance, one may contain nothing but documents from HEW or a new Federal Circular from OMB. The primary purpose of creating these publications-within-a-publication is to provide a detachable booklet that can be easily filed or mailed by itself, should an agency or individual so desire.

How to Order

Subscriptions run $50 per year, $5 per month, and $.75 per single issue. Annual subscribers receive a monthly index free ($8 per year for all other readers). For your subscription or single issue, write:

Superintendent of Documents
Government Printing Office
Washington, D.C. 20402

Reference copies are available for review at Federal Depository Libraries and Federal Information Centers and are usually stocked by large public, college, and law libraries.

Two telephone numbers may be useful to you. Call DIAL-A-REG, 212-523-5022, for highlights of tomorrow's edition of the *Federal Register*. For general inquiries, call 212-523-5240.

Federal
Information Centers

What is the single best centralized source of information when you want a quick answer on a particular aspect of the Federal-government system? In most cases it is the multi-office Federal Information Center operation. If a Federal Information Center can't answer your question outright, it usually has sufficient information resources on hand to refer you to the appropriate office, thus saving you the headache of searching your way through the complex bureaucratic maze.

Following is a list of the Federal Information Centers. Approximately half the cities on the list do not have physical centers per se, but do have a toll-free telephone number connecting you with a center in another city. For example, if you live in Birmington, Alabama, you can dial 322-8591 (which is a local Birmingham number) and reach, via a toll-free tie line, the Federal Information Center in Atlanta, Georgia. Whenever an address is given in a listing, it means that there is an actual center that you can visit, write, or telephone (but in this case, you use the area code and pay the toll, should you place your call from out of town).

ALABAMA:
   Birmingham: 322-8591 (toll-free number to Atlanta, Georgia)
   Mobile: 438-1421 (toll-free number to New Orleans, Louisiana)
ARIZONA:
   Phoenix: (602) 261-3313, Federal Building, 230 North First Avenue, ZIP 85025
   Tucson: 622-1511 (toll-free number to Phoenix, Arizona)

ARKANSAS:
  Little Rock: 378-6177 (toll-free number to Memphis, Tennessee)
CALIFORNIA:
  Los Angeles: (213) 688-3800—Federal Building, 300 North Los Angeles Street, ZIP 90012
  Sacramento: (916) 449-3344—Federal Building, 650 Capitol Mall, ZIP 95814
  San Diego: (714) 293-6030—202 C Street, ZIP 92101
  San Francisco: (415) 556-6600—Federal Building, 450 Golden Gate Avenue, ZIP 94102
  San Jose: 275-7422 (toll-free number to San Francisco, California)
COLORADO:
  Colorado Springs: 471-9491 (toll-free number to Denver, Colorado)
  Denver: (303) 837-3602—Federal Building, 1961 Stout Street, ZIP 80202
  Pueblo: 544-9523 (toll-free number to Denver, Colorado)
CONNECTICUT:
  Hartford: 527-2617 (toll-free number to New York, New York)
  New Haven: 624-4720 (toll-free number to New York, New York)
DISTRICT OF COLUMBIA:
  Washington: (202) 755-8660—Seventh and D Streets, S.W., ZIP 20407
FLORIDA:
  Fort Lauderdale: 522-8531 (toll-free number to Miami, Florida)
  Jacksonville: 354-4756 (toll-free number to St. Petersburg, Florida)
  Miami: (305) 350-4155—Federal Building, 51 S.W. First Avenue, ZIP 33130
  St. Petersburg: (813) 893-3495—Cramer Federal Building, 144 First Avenue South, ZIP 33701
  Tampa: 229-7911 (toll-free number to St. Petersburg, Florida)
  West Palm Beach: 833-7566 (toll-free number to Miami, Florida)
GEORGIA:
  Atlanta: (404) 526-6891—Federal Building, 275 Peachtree Street, NE, ZIP 30303
HAWAII:
  Honolulu: (808) 546-8620—U.S. Post Office, 335 Merchant Street, ZIP 96813
ILLINOIS:
  Chicago: (312) 353-4242—Dirksen Building, 219 South Dearborn Street, 60604
INDIANA:
  Indianapolis: (317) 269-7373— Federal Building, 575 North Pennsylvania, ZIP 46204
IOWA:
  Des Moines: 282-9091 (toll-free number to Omaha, Nebraska)
KANSAS:
  Topeka: 232-7229 (toll-free number to Kansas City, Missouri)
  Wichita: 263-6931 (toll-free number to Kansas City, Missouri)

KENTUCKY:
Louisville: (502) 582-6261— Federal Building, 600 Federal Place, ZIP 40202
LOUISIANA:
New Orleans: (504) 589-6696— Federal Building, 701 Loyola Avenue, ZIP 70113
MARYLAND:
Baltimore: (301) 962-4980—Federal Building, 31 Hopkins Plaza, ZIP 21201
MASSACHUSETTS:
Boston: (617) 223-7121—Kennedy Federal Building, Cambridge Street, ZIP 02203
MICHIGAN:
Detroit: (313) 226-7016—Federal Building, 231 West Lafayette Street, ZIP 48226
MINNESOTA:
Minneapolis: (612) 725-2073—Federal Building, 110 South Fourth Street, ZIP 55401
MISSOURI:
Kansas City: (816) 374-2466—Federal Building, 601 East Twelfth Street, ZIP 64106
St. Joseph: 233-8206 (toll-free number to Kansas City, Missouri)
St. Louis: (314) 425-4106—Federal Building, 1520 Market Street, ZIP 63103
NEBRASKA:
Omaha: (402) 221-3353—Federal Building, 215 North 17th Street, ZIP 68102
NEW JERSEY:
Newark: (201) 645-3600—Federal Building, 970 Broad Street, ZIP 07102
Trenton: 396-4400 (toll-free number to Newark, New Jersey)
NEW MEXICO:
Albuquerque: (505) 766-3091—Federal Building, 500 Gold Avenue, SW, ZIP 87101
Santa Fe: 983-7743 (toll-free number to Albuquerque, New Mexico)
NEW YORK:
Albany: 463-4421 (toll-free number to New York, New York)
Buffalo: (716) 842-5770—Federal Building, 111 West Huron Street, ZIP 14202
New York: (212) 264-4464—Federal Building, 26 Federal Plaza, ZIP 10007
Rochester: 546-5075 (toll-free number to Buffalo, New York)
Syracuse: 476-8545 (toll-free number to Buffalo, New York)
NORTH CAROLINA:
Charlotte: 376-3600 (toll-free number to Atlanta, Georgia)

OHIO:
  Akron: 375-5475 (toll-free number to Cleveland, Ohio)
  Cincinnati: (513) 684-2801—Federal Building, 550 Main Street, ZIP 45202
  Cleveland: (216) 522-4040—Federal Building, 1240 East Ninth Street, ZIP 44199
  Columbus: 221-1014 (toll-free number to Cincinnati, Ohio)
  Dayton: 223-7377 (toll-free number to Cincinnati, Ohio)
  Toledo: 244-8625 (toll-free number to Cleveland, Ohio)
OKLAHOMA:
  Oklahoma City: (405) 231-4868—U.S. Post Office, 201 NW 3rd Street, ZIP 73102
  Tulsa: 584-4193 (toll-free number to Oklahoma City, Oklahoma)
OREGON:
  Portland: (503) 221-2222—Federal Building, 1220 SW Third Avenue, ZIP 97204
PENNSYLVANIA:
  Philadelphia: (215) 597-7042—Federal Building, 600 Arch Street, ZIP 19106
  Pittsburgh: (412) 644-3456—Federal Building, 1000 Liberty Avenue, ZIP 15222
  Scranton: 346-7081 (toll-free number to Philadelphia, Pennsylvania)
RHODE ISLAND:
  Providence: 331-5565 (toll-free number to Boston, Massachusetts)
TENNESSEE:
  Chattanooga: 265-8231 (toll-free number to Memphis, Tennessee)
  Memphis: (901) 534-3285—Davis Federal Building, 167 North Main Street, ZIP 38103
TEXAS:
  Austin: 472-5494 (toll-free number to Houston, Texas)
  Dallas: 749-2131 (toll-free number to Forth Worth, Texas)
  Fort Worth: (817) 334-3624—Lanham Federal Building, 819 Taylor Street, ZIP 76102
  Houston: (713) 226-5711—Federal Building, 515 Rusk Avenue, ZIP 77002
  San Antonio: 224-4471 (toll-free number to Houston, Texas)
UTAH:
  Ogden: 399-1347 (toll-free number to Salt Lake City, Utah)
  Salt Lake City: (801) 524-5353—Federal Building, 125 South State Street, ZIP 84138
WASHINGTON:
  Seattle: (206) 442-0570—Federal Building, 915 Second Avenue, ZIP 98174
  Tacoma: 383-5230 (toll-free number to Seattle, Washington)
WISCONSIN:
  Milwaukee: 271-2273 (toll-free number to Chicago, Illinois)

There are plans to expand the number of Centers even further. For an updated list, write:

> Coordinator
> Federal Information Centers
> General Services Administration
> 18th & F Streets, N.W.
> Washington, D.C., 20405

Federal
Regional Councils

Since its establishment in 1972 by Presidential Executive Order No. 11647, the Federal Regional Council system has been steadily increasing its power and effectiveness—and, consequently, it is becoming more imperative for grant-seekers to understand how and why the relatively new system functions.

Though the FRC system is willing and able to help nongovernmental bodies and individuals, its primary purpose is to serve the needs of the state and local governments by fostering cooperation between the Federal and subnational governments, and by minimizing inconsistencies between two or more programs emanating from different federal agencies. For example, let's suppose a city wishes to undertake a project that requires the assistance of both HUD and HEW, but runs into a snag when it discovers that one policy of HUD is in direct conflict with a HEW regulation. The problem would be resolved, if possible, at a Regional Council meeting.

FRCs also help disseminate to the state and local governments useful decentralized data such as its Budget Information System (BIS) that breaks down federal outlays by state. Still another function is helping coordinate the A-95 Clearinghouse Review System between the Federal and subnational governments.

Because of their pan-agency role in the Federal government, FRC staff members are usually quite effective in steering you to the right agency and program official and in telling you which

STANDARD FEDERAL REGIONS

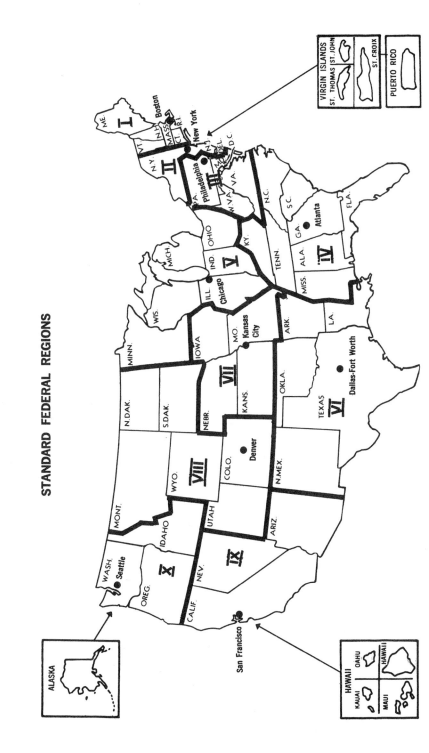

current or upcoming program may be relevant to your needs. It is with these two services that FRCs can be most valuable to nongovernmental bodies and individuals.

The FRC system is divided into ten standard federal administrative regions, each with a headquarter city (indicated by a black dot on the accompanying map). Fortunately, for the sake of consistency, more and more federal agencies—especially the major grant-making ones—are restructuring their regional boundaries to conform to those employed by the FRC system.

Each council's membership comprises eleven regional-level officials, one from the Departments of HEW, HUD, Agriculture, Labor, Interior, Commerce, and Transportation, as well as one from the Environmental Protection Agency, Federal Energy Administration, Community Services Administration, and Law Enforcement Assistance Administration. The President appoints a part-time chairman from the membership. The day-to-day work is administered by a small specialized staff under the supervision of the full-time regional staff director.

Meetings are generally held on the first and third Tuesdays of every month. Representatives from other federal agencies are often invited to attend if an item on the agenda concerns their bailiwick.

Personnel information and the address of each Council is readily available in the *Catalog of Federal Domestic Assistance* and in most government directories, or ask your nearest Federal Information Office.

Please note that the Federal Regional Councils should not be confused with the Federal Executive Boards (FEBs) found in some twenty-five metropolitan areas. FEBs, whose membership consists of the federal field office heads based within a metropolis, are principally concerned with improving coordination within the Federal government.

Federal Circulars

To play the "grant game," you must obviously understand the rules. Many of these rules are spelled out in explicit detail in a series of Federal Circulars, usually referred to as either "Circular A-s" or "FMCs."* Their primary purpose is to set uniform administrative standards for all funding agencies and, as a result, may directly or indirectly affect you. These standards determine grant budget revisions, indirect costs, reporting and cost-sharing requirements, and much more. Before circulars came into effect, grant requirements varied so greatly from agency to agency that the recipient was often left with a hazy understanding of what was expected of him or her.

Because the circulars delineate the requirements grant-seekers must follow, it is suggested that grant-seekers (especially those interested in large-scale grants) understand the guidelines stated in those circulars pertaining to their particular program.

Determining which circulars are relevant to your project is not so difficult: consult the *Federal Register,* the *Catalog of*

---

* The responsibility for preparing and administering certain Federal Circulars was originally in the hands of the Office of Management and Budget (OMB). In 1973 this responsibility was transferred to the General Services Administration (GSA), and then, in 1976, transferred back to OMB. This back-and-forth movement of administrative responsibility has caused some confusion in the prefixes given to Federal Circulars: some are designated "FMCs" and others "Circular A-s." If a Federal Circular has a "Federal Management Circular" designation such as "FMC 74-7," it was instituted during the GSA administrative period. If, on the other hand, a circular has an "A-" designation, such as "A-95," it was instituted during either the first or current OMB administrative period. To eliminate this confusion, OMB is considering changing all FMC designations into its own "Circular A-" prefix system.

Federal Domestic Assistance, or the official in charge of the program. The last source is the best because he or she has the most current facts—and may be able to give enough answers so that you won't have to peruse all the Circulars yourself.

Following is a brief description of those circulars that tend to be most relevant to grant-seekers.

Circular A-40

Applies to: Federal departments, agencies, and commissions (and often grantees and contractors) gathering information to satisfy a federal standard or need. *Purpose:* To reduce the administrative chore demanded of individuals and organizations when they reply to questionnaires, surveys, applications, and other data-gathering instruments employed either by the government or by a private unit on behalf of the government. Also, Circular A-40 fosters consistency and cost-effectiveness on the compilation of statistical data concerning the public.

Circular A-46

Applies to: Federal agencies, their private contractors, and grant recipients. *Purpose:* To provide uniform standards for surveying and disseminating federal statistics.

Circular A-84

Applies to: All federal agencies. *Purpose:* To acquaint agencies with the required procedures for gathering data on federal outlays on a geographical basis.

Circular A-85

Applies to: Federal agencies whose programs affect subnational governments. *Purpose:* To allow the chief executives of state and local governments to review, prior to its going into effect, any agency regulation directly pertaining to their jurisdiction.

Circular A-89

Applies to: All federal agencies offering domestic assistance. *Purpose:* To provide necessary guidelines for the preparation and issuance of the *Catalog of Federal Domestic Assistance.*

Circular A-90

Applies to: All federal agencies funding information systems involving state and local governments. *Purpose:* To establish an efficient intergovernmental communication system that reduces, for example, the chances of duplicating prepared information.

Circular A-95: See Appendix D.
TC-1082 (Also known as: Treasury Circular 1082)

Applies to: Federal agencies administering grants-in-aid to state and local governments. *Purpose:* To help make sure that state and local governments are kept informed on federal grants-in-aid that might affect them. For more details, see the "State Central Information Reception Agencies" section on page 186.

Circular A-105

Applies to: Federal (but not regulatory) domestic agencies. *Purpose:* To make the regional boundaries and headquarter cities of the various federal agencies more consistent with each other by encouraging these agencies to reorganize their regions into the ten standard regions adopted by the Federal Regional Councils (see map on page 146).

Circular A-110

Applies to: Agencies administering aid to nonprofit organizations such as colleges, universities, and hospitals. *Purpose:* To encourage administrative consistency among federal agencies by establishing uniform requirements for nonprofit grantees to follow on such matters as accounting and property management. Because this responsibility is placed in the hands of the grantee, the federal agency's administrative paperwork is reduced.

Circular A-111

Applies to: Heads of federal departments and agencies. *Purpose:* To establish administrative policies for federally assisted joint-funding programs going to state and local governments as well as to nonprofit organizations.

FMC 73-1

Applies to: Federal agencies. *Purpose:* To help ensure that Executive Branch departments and agencies understand and follow the instructions mandated by Federal Circulars.

FMC 73-2

Applies to: Federal agencies. *Purpose:* To refine auditing procedures and practices of federal programs, as well as to encourage early audits of new or altered programs. It requires that all federal agencies maintain an audit program, comply with established standards, and prepare audit reports.

FMC 73-3

Applies to: Federal and private agencies executing federally funded research. *Purpose:* To establish guidelines for determining the dollar amount (if any) for which an organization conducting federally funded research is responsible.

FMC 73-6

Applies to: Federal agencies and educational institutions receiving federal funds. *Purpose:* To determine policies for indirect cost rates and auditing procedures with educational institutions, and to alleviate the burden placed on them when forced to comply with the varying guidelines of several agencies.

FMC 73-7

Applies to: Federal agencies and educational institutions awarded research grants or contracts. *Purpose:* To establish standard policies and thereby promote consistency among federal agencies when administering research grants and contracts to educational institutions.

FMC 73-8

Applies to: Federal agencies. *Purpose:* To determine (through the use of recognized accounting principles) the costs of educational services developed by educational institutions and made possible by federal grants and contracts.

FMC 74-3

Applies to: Federal agencies. *Purpose:* To determine procedures for federal agencies to follow in the event a pre-awarded contract proposal is under protest.

FMC 74-4

Applies to: Federal agencies administering grants and contracts to state and local governments. *Purpose:* To provide uniform principles intended to assist federal agencies in ascertaining direct and indirect costs for grants and contracts administered to state and local governments. The application of these uniform standards encourages efficiency and eliminates friction between the grantee and the acting federal agency.

FMC 74-5

Applies to: Federal agencies and contractors operating automatic data-processing equipment (ADPE) under a government contract. *Purpose:* To stipulate the regulations governing the use of ADPE in programs funded by government contracts. This includes work performed under cost-reimbursement and subcontracts as well.

FMC 74-7 (replaces A-102)

Applies to: Federal agencies. *Purpose:* Previously, many federal agencies had different and sometimes contradictory grant standards for state and local governments to follow. This caused a needless administrative headache. FMC 74-7 now requires that federal agencies adopt uniform standards when administering grants-in-aid programs to the state and local government. The standards deal with financial management and reports, grant payments, matching shares, and budget revision procedures, among other items.

FMC 74-8 (replaces A-103)

Applies to: Federal agencies administering programs that involve the displacement of people, businesses, or farm operations. *Purpose:* To establish that all federal agencies funding programs involving the relocation of persons, businesses, or farm operations be responsible for related costs incurred in the displacement process. Stipulations are also made for nonprofit organizations.

FMC 74-9

Applies to: Federal agencies. *Purpose:* To encourage federal agencies to maintain control over their funds by ensuring a proper relationship between the monies the agencies spend and the funds appropriated by Congress.

FMC Dating Code

The prefixes given to each of the above Federal Management Circulars indicate the year and order in which it was issued. FMC 73-2, for example, was the second Federal Management Circular issued in 1973.

Free Copies and Assistance

For free copies of any of the above Circulars, write to the following address (along with a brief substantiation of your need for them):

> Publications Division
> Office of Management and Budget
> Room G236
> New Executive Office Building
> Washington, D.C. 20503

If you have an unanswered question pertaining to a particular circular under the direct jurisdiction of OMB, contact:

> Financial Management Branch
> Budget Review Division
> Office of Management and Budget
> Room 7225
> New Executive Office Building
> Washington, D.C. 20503

OTHER SOURCES OF
Information

Academic Research Information System (ARIS)

This private organization publishes three *Aris Funding Messenger* periodicals, each of which gives funding data in a different field: the monthly *Medical,* the monthly *Social and Natural Sciences Report,* and the nine-times-a-year *Creative Arts and Humanities.* Annual subscriptions run $84 for the first two publications and $63 for the third one. Write the publisher:

> Academic Research Information System
> Pacific Medical Center
> 230 Clay Street
> San Francisco, California 94115

American Association of Fund-Raising Counsel (AAFRC)

Most of the large professional fund-raising counseling services belong to this trade organization. Though its principal thrust is in keeping its members and publication readers current on the private, as opposed to public, grant-giving sector, AAFRC does to a limited degree delve into fedeal-agency funding programs. For descriptive literature on AAFRC, write:

> American Association of Fund-Raising Counsel
> 500 Fifth Avenue
> New York, New York 10036

Annual Register of Grant Support

The *Register* is a mammoth 600+-page hardcover directory prepared principally for fund-seeking individuals as opposed to organizations. It details over fifteen hundred funding sources, including various government agencies, corporations, associations, fraternal organizations, and foundations. Collectively, these sources fund nearly one million scholarships, grants, awards, prizes, and other types of individual-oriented financial aid. Entries are categorized by field of interest. Four quick-reference indexes (subject, geographic, organizational, and personnel) help you find the appropriate entries. One of the directory's chief drawbacks is caused by its success: so many grant-seekers use the book that many of the listed funding sources are inundated with funding requests, thereby creating competition out of proportion to the number of dollars available. Another shortcoming: the directory (despite its size) is far from being comprehensive. Nevertheless, the *Register* is the best single national source of funding data for individuals. You'll find the *Register* at practically all large public and college libraries. To order your own copy, mail $52.50 to the publisher:

Marquis Who's Who, Inc.
200 East Ohio Street
Chicago, Illinois 60611

Bill Status System

If a pending legislative bill concerns you, it is a good idea to keep abreast of its progress in Congress so that you can better plan for the future.

Fortunately, there is a quick, easy, and free way to learn the current status of a bill under consideration in Congress. All you need to do is to call a special congressional "hotline" telephone number: 202-225-1772. Simply give the operator sufficient data to identify the bill (the bill number or title—or perhaps a combination of identifying factors such as the bill's subject, sponsor, cosponsor, referral committee, and/or introduction date). Sitting in front of a video display terminal, the operator retrieves from the computer in a matter of seconds the information you requested. For example: "Yesterday the Senate Committee on Government Operations approved its version of the bill 17 to 11." The complete step-by-step, committee-by-committee history of the bill can also be quickly retrieved for you.

You can also obtain the same bill-status information in printed form by writing to:

> Bill Status System
> House Information Systems
> Committee on House Administration
> U.S. Congress
> Washington, D.C. 20515

For a free 28-page pamphlet describing the Bill Status System, write to the above address and request "The Bill Status System" publication.

Brakeley, John Price Jones

This is one of the large private firms providing a broad spectrum of fund-raising (including grant-seeking) consulting services. For information, write:

> Brakeley, John Price Jones
> 6 East 43rd Street
> New York, New York 10017

Budget of the United States Government

Each year the President submits to Congress his budget for the upcoming fiscal year. This information is published annually in *The Budget of the United States Government* and its three companion volumes, *The United States Budget in Brief,* the *Appendix,* and *Special Analysis.*

Though the proposed budget figures presented in these publications represent the President's suggested budget and not the final amounts voted on by Congress, these figures provide you with a valuable interim source of data until the congressional figures are known. This interim data will help you predict the direction and scope of future federal funding.

Of the four publications in the set, *The Budget of the United States Government* ($3.45) is the keystone. It gives you a somewhat detailed summation and overview of the proposed budget, the current year's budget, and the previous year's budget. Also presented is general background information such as the President's Budget Message. Though the figures published in this book are useful to you as a grant-seeker, be forewarned that you can't precisely update your *Catalog of Federal Domestic Assistance* with the proposed budget figures even if these amounts were to be passed into law unchanged because the *Budget* and *Catalog* books generally use different accounting categories. For instance, a single *Budget* book account may fund several separate programs listed in the *Catalog.*

The United States Budget in Brief ($1.15) presents a less-detailed overview than the *Budget* book. If you have only a limited amount of time to devote to studying the U.S. budget, perhaps you can get by with this volume alone.

The *Appendix* ($19.20) contains in-depth details such as the proposed budget figures for each specific account, the proposed wording of the funding laws, and the work descriptions. Rather than investing in this book, you might consider copying the figures and Xeroxing the pages relevant to your project.

Special Analysis ($2.70) gives you economic and financial analyses on topics such as the effects of federal debt, tax expenditures, and Executive Branch employment. Also analyzed are select key federal-program areas, including education and health—and the envisioned impact of federal activity such as aid to state and local governments.

You can find reference copies of all four publications at Federal Depository Libraries and Federal Information Centers —and sometimes at large public and college libraries. Individual copies may be purchased at GPO bookstores or by writing:

> Superintendent of Documents
> Government Printing Office
> Washington, D.C. 20402

Businessman's Guide to Washington

A clearly written 408-page book for executives wishing to seek services, contracts, or financial and information assistance from the Legislative or Executive Branches. Cost: $8.95 hardcover and $4.50 paperback. Write the publisher:

> Macmillan Publishing Company
> 866 Third Avenue
> New York, New York 10022

Center for Community Change

Low-income and minority community organizations can gain valuable technical assistance—including a newsletter and a series of booklets on grant development—from the Center for Community Change, a nonprofit organization. For the details, write:

> Center for Community Change
> 1000 Wisconsin Avenue, N.W.
> Washington, D.C. 20007

Cities

City officials can subscribe to a number of publications carrying pertinent grant-related news:

The biweekly *NLC Washington Report.* Annual subscriptions run $40 for NLC members and $70 for nonmembers. Write:

> National League of Cities
> 1620 I Street, N.W.
> Washington, D.C. 20006

The various publications from the International City Management Association. These include the semimonthly *ICMA Newsletter,* the monthly *Public Management* magazine, and the *Municipal Year Book.* For descriptive literature, write:

> ICMA
> 1140 Connecticut Avenue, N.W.
> Washington, D.C. 20036

The periodic *Legislative Bulletin* and the monthly *CUED Commentary.* A combined subscription runs $15 per year. Write the publisher:

National Council for Urban Economic Development
1620 I Street, N.W.
Washington, D.C. 20006

Many other trade publications—such as the monthly *Nation's Cities* magazine—also occasionally print grant-related news.

Code of Federal Regulations (CFR)

A single volume containing all the existing and new federal regulations would be prohibitively bulky, measuring several feet in width. Consequently the government has divided the regulations into some fifty separate titles covering broad subject areas, such as agriculture. Each title is updated at least once a year. (The source of information is the *Federal Register*.) The entire CFR set comprises over one hundred volumes (some titles are multi-volumed) and costs $350. Individual volumes cost, on the average, several dollars each and are sometimes available at federal bookstores. To order, or for a complete title and price list, write:

> Superintendent of Documents
> U.S. Government Printing Office
> Washington, D.C. 20402

However, if you wish the specific regulations affecting a particular grant program, it is often best to request the information directly from the official in charge of the program, who, in most cases, is happy to oblige you. In this way you save yourself the bother of sifting through the various CFRs, a time-consuming process.

Commerce Business Daily (CBD)

While of minimal value to grant-seekers, the *Commerce Business Daily (CBD)* is a gold mine of information for contract-seekers.

Basically, *CBD,* a Department of Commerce publication, is a Sears, Roebuck Catalog in reverse, since it lists items to be purchased rather than sold. It is the official vehicle for notifying the public of virtually everything the U.S. Government plans to buy—thus giving everyone, at least in theory, an equal chance to submit a bid.

Announced bidding opportunities include those for the procurement of equipment, services, and material or research through contracts. Also included within *CBD* is information on subcontracting leads, contract awards, sales of surplus property, and foreign business opportunities. By law, almost all Requests for Proposals (RFPs) of $5,000 or more and awarded contracts exceeding $25,000 must be published in the *Commerce Business Daily*.

The entries concerning contract-seekers will usually briefly describe such specifications as the work to be done, application and project deadline dates, the contractor's eligibility requirements, and whether you can request the RFP directly or whether you must first prove your qualifications before receiving the RFP. The RFP, once you receive it, spells out the purchase specifications in greater detail than found in the *Commerce Business Daily*. Be prepared for tedious reading, as *CBD*'s wording is terse, abbreviations are rampant, and footnotes are freely used—sometimes to the point where readability is severely impaired. Always save Monday's edition as many of the footnotes in the Tuesday through Friday editions are explained exclusively in that first-of-the-week edition.

Commerce Business Daily is sold only on an annual subscription basis. To order, mail $80 for a second-class-mail subscription or $105 for a first-class-mail subscription to:

> Commerce Business Daily publication
> Superintendent of Documents
> U.S. Government Printing Office
> Washington, D.C. 20402

Reference copies are available at Federal Depository Libraries and Federal Information Centers—and at most large public and college libraries.

Congressional Committee Publications

Many Congressional committtes keep the public up to date on their activities by publishing documents such as press releases and newsletters. Be sure to ask these committees to send you any of their published material that may be relevant to your program, as this printed information is often timely. Another way to obtain these congressional committee documents is through the office of your senator or congressman.

Congressional Directory

This is a fact-filled 1,000+-page reference book published annually by the U.S. Government. Besides providing biographical sketches of senators and representatives, the directory lists congressional staff members, congressional committees, historical statistical data on Congress, key Executive Branch officials including those from the departments and independent agencies, key officials of the Judiciary Branch, members of the Foreign Service and Diplomatic Corps, accredited members of the press galleries, congressional districts (state-by-state maps are given), and much more. Cost: $6.50 for the paperback, $8.50 for the hardcover, and $12.95 for the indexed hardcover edition, Order from:

> Superintendent of Documents
> U.S. Government Printing Office
> Washington, D.C. 20402

Congressional Quarterly Weekly Report

For those who can afford the $507-per-year subscription rate, the privately published *Congressional Quarterly Weekly Report* is an excellent source of timely background information on pending and proposed legislation. The subscription fee includes ninety-day cumulative indexes, a 1,500-page *Almanac* of last year's congressional events, and a telephone research service. Write the publisher:

> Congressional Quarterly
> 1414 22nd Street, N.W.
> Washington, D.C. 20037

Congressional Record

Published every day that Congress is in session, the official *Congressional Record* is an excellent source on data on the status of legislation in Congress. However, it is much too voluminous for all but the largest of grant- and contract-seeking organizations to digest on a daily basis. It transcribes verbatim almost every word spoken on the congressional floors as well as numerous written records that are printed at the request of senators and congressmen. Annual subscriptions may be obtained for $45 from the U.S. Government Printing Office. You may be able to get a free subscription (or at least free copies of germane issues) from your congressman. Individual review copies are available at Federal Depository Libraries and Federal Information Centers—and at some large public and college libraries.

Congressional Staff Directory

A well-organized 1,000-page hardcover volume that lists and gives brief biographical data on senators and congressmen—and on their key staff members. (It is this last feature of the book that proves to be of unique value.) This annual privately published edition also lists and gives biographies on key Executive Branch personnel. Cost: $19.50. Write the publisher:

Congressional Staff Directory
P.O. Box 62
Mount Vernon, Virginia 22121

Contracting for Purchase of Services

Should you be involved in seeking government contracts, you may wish to purchase a copy of the *Contracting for Purchase of Services* paperback published by the University of Southern California. Though it is written with the contract-seeker from the social welfare field in mind, it clearly defines and illustrates many of the fine points of the general Federal-government contract-seeking process and, as such, makes a fine reference book for any contract-seeker's library. For a copy and its addendum, send $5.00 to:

Contracting for Purchase of Services
Regional Research Institute in Social Welfare
USC School of Social Work
Los Angeles, California 90007

Copies of Congressional Bills

For a free single copy of any pending or enacted congressional bill, send a self-addressed label to the Documents Room of the appropriate house:

U.S. Senate
Washington, D.C. 20510
or
House of Representatives
Washington, D.C. 20515

Cultural Directory

Targeted for grant-seekers in the cultural field, the *Cultural Directory* is a descriptive guide to over 250 federal and quasi-governmental funding programs for individual artists and cultural organizations. This 340-page paperback also describes several dozen major cultural advisory groups and summarizes some of the pertinent laws and regulations affecting the grant-seeker. Cost: $4.00 per copy. To order, write the publisher:

> ACA Publications
> Associated Councils of the Arts
> 570 Seventh Avenue
> New York, New York 10018

Depository Libraries

Some 1,200 public and college libraries have been appointed by the U.S. Government to stock federal publications and to make them permanently available for public use. If one of these Depository Libraries is classified as "selective," it means that it selects and retains only those publications that fall under specified categories best serving the needs of its users. Depository Libraries are especially useful in two cases: when you can't wait for the Superintendent of Documents to process your order, and when the publication is out of print and no longer available from the Superintendent of Documents. For a free list of locations write:

> Library
> Public Documents Department
> U.S. Government Printing Office
> Washington, D.C. 20402

District of Columbia Telephone Directory

The Washington metropolitan area "white-page" telephone directory can be a time-saver if you frequently call or write a variety of people based in the nation's capital. Here's a tip: you can usually obtain a free copy of the latest edition simply by requesting one from the business office of your local telephone company. (In most cities the number you dial is 811.) Allow one or two weeks for delivery.

Directory of Key Government Personnel

Hill and Knowlton, Inc., the world's largest public relations firm, publishes this 100+-page, 4 × 6″ vest-pocket guide giving the names, titles, addresses, and telephone numbers of key government officials in the Executive, Judiciary, and Legislative Branches. Copies are given gratis. Write, preferably on your letterhead, to:

> Directory of Key Government Personnel
> Hill and Knowlton, Inc.
> 633 Third Avenue
> New York, New York 10017

Education Funding Research Council (EFRC)

EFRC, a private service, supplies data on education-oriented federal aid via these vehicles: *Education Funding News* (a weekly newsletter summarizing current and upcoming federal education funding programs); *Congressional Boxscore* (a periodic status report of educational bills working their way through Congress); "Washington Hotline" (information by phone); "Legislative Status Report"; "VIP Proposal Delivery" (delivered by a messenger); "Retrieval Service" (published material is gathered for you). The full service runs $186 per year. For $96 per year, you receive only the *Education Funding News* and *Congressional Boxscore*. For $19.95 (soft cover) or $24.95 (hard cover) you'll receive the annual *Federal Funding Guide for Elementary and Secondary Education* book detailing over one hundred educational-aid programs. For full details write:

Education Funding Research Council
752 National Press Building, N.W.
Washington, D.C. 20045

Encyclopedia of Associations

Trade organizations within your field are among the best sources of information on specialized government-grant activity. If you are not familiar with all organizations within your discipline, the *Encyclopedia of Associations* is an excellent set of directories, comprising three oversized volumes. The first, *National Organizations of the U.S.* ($64), is in all probability the most valuable one for your purposes. Its 1,500+ pages describe some fifteen thousand organizations and contain an extensive quick-reference index. Volume 2, *Geographic & Executive Index* ($45), has approximately 750 pages indexing the associations by state and city and their executives alphabetically. Volume #3, *New Associations & Projects* ($55), updates Volume 1 between editions. Most large libraries have copies of the encyclopedia, especially Volume I. To order, write the publisher:

Gale Research Company
Book Tower
Detroit, Michigan 48226

Encyclopedia of Governmental Advisory Organizations

One of the most effective ways of keeping abreast of what federal Executive and Legislative Branches are planning to do in your field is to establish a dialogue with organizations that advise the various U.S. Government units. The prime reference book on this subject is the *Encyclopedia of Governmental Advisory Organizations*. This 668-page oversized hardcover book furnishes vital details such as the history, authority, types of programs, and membership of over twenty-five hundred advisory groups. The entries are divided into ten topical sections and are well indexed, enabling you to locate quickly the organizations relevant to your project. The encyclopedia is available at many large libraries—or you may order the book and its series of semiannual updates for $75 directly from the publisher:

> Gale Research Company
> Book Tower
> Detroit, Michigan 48226

Federal Assistance Programs Retrieval System (FAPRS)

The U.S. Department of Agriculture (USDA) has developed a new computerized grant-information system that holds great promise. While FAPRS was originally designed to serve rural communities, it was such a good concept that it is now being gradually expanded to serve federal grant-seekers in general.

Basically, you describe to USDA's Rural Development Service your organization and its funding needs. USDA then feeds your data into a computer (that it is hoped) spews forth a list of federal programs offering you funding potential. The print-out is keyed to the U.S. Government's official five-digit program code numbers, thereby enabling you to look up the details of a program quickly in the *Catalog of Federal Domestic Assistance*.

The cost to you is either free or a token amount, depending on the decision by the FAPRS official. For further information, write:

> FAPRS Administrator
> Rural Development Service
> USDA
> Washington, D.C. 20250

Federal Contracts Report

This weekly publication contains pertinent, well-researched data for government grant- as well as contract-seekers. The

Report's staff does much of the legwork for you by gathering and summarizing recent and planned policy and legal decisions made by Congress, the court system, grantor agencies, and Executive Branch service agencies such as the General Accounting Office (GAO). A one-year subscription runs $270. Write:

> Federal Contracts Report
> Bureau of National Affairs, Inc.
> 1231 25th Street, N.W.
> Washington, D.C. 20037

Federal Notes

Researched and written for grant- and contract-seekers in educational, biomedical, and scientific fields, the twice-monthly *Federal Notes* newsletter digests pertinent information such as new programs and pending legislation. Subscriptions run $60 for one year, $110 for two years. Write the publisher:

> Federal Notes
> P.O. Box 986
> Saratoga, California 95070

Federal Regional Councils (FRCs)

Among their many other duties, FRCs provide decentralized regional data on federal funding programs and are often in good position to direct you to the proper funding sources for your particular project. For a fuller discussion of the FRC system see page 145.

Fund Raising Management

The chief value of this commercial trade publication to a grant-seeker is in providing up-to-date information on the types of business services being offered to fund raisers. For example, this glossy bimonthly journal overflows with ads promoting new direct-mail methods, accounting systems, and consulting services. As for "how-to-win-a-grant" type articles, they are few and far between. Subscriptions run $10 per year. Write the publisher:

>Hoke Communications, Inc.
>224 Seventh Street
>Garden City, New York 11530

Federal Research Report

This report furnishes information on research-oriented federal grants and contracts. Deadline dates are included. Subscriptions for this weekly newsletter run $48.00 for one year, $85.00 for two years, and $115.00 for three years. Write the publisher:

>Federal Research Report
>P.O. Box 1067
>Blair Station
>Silver Spring, Maryland 20910

Funding Sources Clearinghouse (FSC)

One of the best services for grant-seekers is provided by Funding Sources Clearinghouse, a nonprofit organization.

FSC's specialty is helping you pinpoint high potential government, foundation, and corporate funding sources by using its extensive data banks. Once the computer produces the initial list of high potential candidates, the number is pruned to the most promising five or ten funding sources by a human being, a Funding Sources Clearinghouse staff member.

The annual FSC membership fee is $250 and entitles you to:

Custom project-grant searches (at $25 each)
Funding prospect reports (at $5 each)
Biographical profiles on foundation officials (at $1 each)
Foundation reference sets
Consultation (on proposal writing, et cetera)
And more.

Some of the above services are available to nonmembers as well.

For descriptive literature, write:

> Funding Sources Clearinghouse
> 2600 Bancroft Way
> Berkeley, California 94704

Fund Raising Institute (FRI)

FRI publishes *Capital Ideas,* a three-volume guide to capital fund raising. Most of the 1,020 pages are devoted to reprints of material used for a wide variety of campaigns. Cost: $75. FRI also offers for $35 per year a Monthly Portfolio subscription service that provides you with newsletters, bulletins, and evaluations of fund-raising letters. Write:

> Fund Raising Institute
> P.O. Box 122
> Plymouth Meeting, Pennsylvania 19462

Georgetown University Workshop

A grantsmanship and proposal development workshop lasting several days is conducted in Washington, D.C. by Georgetown University. Tuition is $200.00. For a free brochure, write:

> SSCE
> Georgetown University
> Washington, D.C. 20057

Government Information Services (GIS)

GIS is a private organization serving local governmental units by supplying current data on local government-oriented federal aid. It conveys this information via these vehicles: *Local Government Funding Report* (biweekly newsletter summarizing current and upcoming aid programs); *Federal Register Report* (biweekly newsletter summarizing relevant items in the *Federal Register*); *Congressional Boxscore* (a periodic report of relevant bills working their way through Congress); *Federal Funding Guide for Local Governments* (a 300+-page book giving "how to" information plus details on over one hundred aid programs for state and local governments); "Washington Hotline" (information by phone): "VIP Proposal Delivery Service" (delivered by a messenger); "Retrieval Service" (a material-gathering service). The full service runs $186 per year. For $96 a year, you receive only the first three publications. For $14.95, you get the *Federal Funding Guide for Local Governments* in the soft-cover edition. GIS also conducts seminars. For full details write:

Government Information Services
752 National Press Building, N.W.
Washington, D.C. 20045

Government R&D Report

This commercial firm publishes information on federal programs aiding research and development projects. Subscriptions for this bi-monthly pamphlet-format newsletter run $45 for six months, $80 for one year, and $145 for two years. Write the publisher:

Government R&D Report
MIT Station
P.O. Box 284
Cambridge, Massachusetts 02139

GPO Bookstores

The U.S. Government Printing Office operates about two dozen bookstores spread across the country. With the exception of the main bookstore in Washington, D.C., these outlets tend to stock only the most popular titles and do not sell the subscription-type publications.

ATLANTA, GEORGIA:
Federal Office Building, 275 Peachtree Street, N.E.
BIRMINGHAM, ALABAMA:
2121 8th Avenue North
BOSTON, MASSACHUSETTS:
John F. Kennedy Federal Building
CANTON,OHIO:
201 Cleveland Avenue, S.W.
CHICAGO, ILLINOIS:
Everett McKinley Dirksen Building, 219 South Dearborn Street
CLEVELAND, OHIO:
Federal Building, 1240 East 9th Street
DALLAS, TEXAS:
New Federal Building, 1100 Commerce Street
DENVER, COLORADO:
Federal Building, 1961 Stout Street
DETROIT, MICHIGAN:
Federal Office Building, 231 West Lafayette Boulevard
JACKSONVILLE, FLORIDA:
Federal Building, 400 West Bay Street
KANSAS CITY, MISSOURI:
Federal Building, 601 East 12th Street
LOS ANGELES, CALIFORNIA:
Federal Building, 300 North Los Angeles Street
MILWAUKEE, WISCONSIN:
Federal Building, 517 East Wisconsin Avenue
NEW YORK, NEW YORK:
Federal Office Building, 26 Federal Plaza
PHILADELPHIA, PENNSYLVANIA:
Federal Office Building, 600 Arch Street
SAN FRANCISCO, CALIFORNIA:
Federal Building, 450 Golden Gate Avenue
SEATTLE, WASHINGTON:
Federal Office Building, 915 Second Avenue
WASHINGTON, D.C.
(six locations): Main Bookstore, 710 North Capitol Street; Com-

merce Department, 4th and E Streets, N.W.; James H. Forrestal Building, 1000 Independence Avenue, S.W.; Pentagon Building, Main Concourse; State Department, 21st and C Streets, N.W.; USIA, 1776 Pennsylvania Avenue, N.W.

GPO Individual Select Bibliographies

The U.S. Government Printing Office has recently begun to compile and release (free) a series of bibliographies on available government publications in selected subject areas. Since the list of subject areas is currently growing and changing, we suggest you write directly to the GPO for its latest list in order to determine whether one of its bibliographies coincides with your field of interest. Write:

> Individual Subject Bibliographies
> Superintendent of Documents
> U.S. Government Printing Office
> Washington, D.C. 20402

If there is no bibliography match-up, or if you want the latest available list of new publications, consider using the *GPO Monthly Catalog* (see below).

GPO Monthly Catalog

The U.S. Government Printing Office prepares a monthly 100+-page catalog listing virtually all the new (and some old) publications issued by all federal governmental bodies. Since these publications cover a wide range of fields, chances are that some relate to your discipline. Considering that most of these government publications are free or relatively low-priced, the $45.00 annual subscription price for the *Monthly Catalog* may be a sound investment for some organizations. (If you are unsure, order a single monthly issue for $3.25.) A semiannual index comes free with each subscription. To order, write:

Monthly Catalog
Superintendent of Documents
U.S. Government Printing Office
Washington, D.C. 20402

GPO Selected U.S. Government Publications

Far less extensive than the GPO *Monthly Catalog* (see above), this monthly pamphlet describes a limited number of new publications selected on the basis of anticipated public interest. A convenient order form is included. You can receive a free continuous subscription by writing:

Selected U.S. Government Publications
Superintendent of Documents
U.S. Government Printing Office
Washington, D.C. 20402

Grant Development Institute

This Colorado-based firm markets its Successful Grantsmanship Kit, comprising three publications telling you how to secure foundation, corporate, and government grants. Cost: $21. Grant Development Institute also conducts seminars for grant-seekers. For descriptive literature, write:

Grant Development Institute
2525 West Main Street
Littleton, Colorado 80120

Grants

Grants: How to Find Out About Them and What to Do Next is one of the best introductory books in the field and, as such, is a worthy edition to any grant-seeker's library. Virginia White's 354-page hardcover volume covers government, foundation, and corporate grants. Don't expect to find a detailed list of funding sources—that's not her purpose. Her goal is to teach you the expertise of pinpointing those sources and tell you how to conduct your campaign. Cost: $19.50. Write the publisher:

Plenum Press
227 West 17th Street
New York, New York 10011

Grants and Awards Available to American Writers

For a copy of this 64-page paperback, mail $2 to the publisher:

P.E.N. American Center
156 Fifth Avenue
New York, New York 10010

Grantsmanship Center

Since its inception in 1972, the nonprofit Grantsmanship Center has been helping train grant-seekers by means of two vehicles:

Grantsmanship Center News: This periodical is filled with well-written how-to and background-type articles that are educational for all but the experienced grant-seeker. Subscriptions run $15 per year (six issues).

Workshops: Week-long training seminars for up to twenty-two participants are conducted in large cities across the country. Geared more for the neophyte and intermediate grant-seeker than for the experienced one, these workshops cover all the basics in winning grants from both the public and private sectors. Enrollment fee: $295 per person.

For a subscription to the *News,* or for further information on the workshops, write:

The Grantsmanship Center
1015 West Olympic Boulevard
Los Angeles, California 90015

Grantsmanship Is Never Having to Say You're Broke

This booklet is designed for grant-seekers in the drug-abuse field. For a copy, mail $1.25 to the publisher:

National Drug Abuse Materials Distribution Center
P.O. Box 398
McLean, Virginia 22101

Grants Register

The individual grant-seeker is the intended user of the *Grants Register,* a 764-page hardcover directory. It is similar to the *Annual Register of Grants Support* in purpose, but it is smaller in content and has a much broader geographical scope: all English-speaking countries. Most large public and college libraries stock a reference copy. For your own copy, send $25.00 to the publisher:

St. Martin's Press
175 Fifth Avenue
New York, New York 10010

Guide to Federal Programs

Written for grant-seekers in the historic-preservation field, *Guide to Federal Programs* describes over 200 federal funding programs, services, and activities. For a copy of this oversized 400-page paperback, mail $8.00 plus $4.50 for its supplement to the publisher.

National Trust for Historic Preservation
740–748 Jackson Place, N.W.
Washington, D.C. 20006

Iuman Resources Network

This nonprofit organization has compiled four well-researched paperback books under the series title *How to get Money for.* . . They include *Education, Fellowships and Scholarships* ($5.95); *Conservation and Community Development* ($5.95); *Youth, the Elderly, the Handicapped, Women, and Civil Liberies* ($7.95); *Arts and Humanities, Drug and Alcohol Abuse, and Health* ($5.95). Each volume provides the grant-seeker with pertinent information such as name, address, deadline date, and description of available funds. The entries are listed by subject area, then broken down geographically. A hardcover edition combining all four books can be purchased for $39.95. To order, write the publisher:

Chilton Book Company
Chilton Way
Radnor, Pennsylvania 19089

nstitute for Fund-Raising

Foundation and Government Grant and Proposal Preparation seminars, lasting two days, are periodically conducted in Chicago, Los Angeles, and New York by the Institute for Fund-Raising. Tuition is $245. For descriptive literature write:

Institute for Fund-Raising
717 Castro Street
San Francisco, California 94114

Lawson Associates

Douglas M. Lawson Associates is a private, full-service fund raising consulting firm. For information, write:

Douglas M. Lawson Associates
39 East 51st Street
New York, New York 10022

Leisure Information Service

Public- and private-sector grants in the leisure field are ana lyzed and summarized in *Fund Development & Technical As sistance Report,* a biweekly newsletter. Subscriptions run $4 per year. Write the publisher:

Leisure Information Service
729 Delaware Avenue, S.W.
Washington, D.C. 20024

Library of Congress

A subdivision of the Library of Congress, the Congression Research Service has prepared a short introductory pamphle entitled *Federal Assistance Programs: How to Get Informatio About Them and Apply for Assistance.* It is available free fror your congressman.

LRC-W Newsbriefs

Published by an arm of the Lutheran Council in Americ the monthly *LRC-W Newsbriefs* describes major public- an private-sector funding opportunities. While the material is re searched and compiled principally for the funding needs of var ous Protestant churches, it is sufficiently broad in subject scop to be of value to many nonreligious organizations as well. Categorized subjects run, for example, from arts and humanities to the environment. Subscriptions cost $50 per year. Write:

> Lutheran Resources Commission—Washington
> Dupont Circle Building
> 1346 Connecticut Avenue, N.W.
> Washington, D.C. 20036

Marts & Lundy

Marts & Lundy is one of the large private firms offering a wide range of fund-raising consulting services to fund-seeking clients. For literature, write:

> Marts & Lundy
> 521 Fifth Avenue
> New York, New York 10017

Museum Guide to Federal Programs

Any museum seeking government grants should consider buying a copy of this well-organized 150+-page loose-leaf book. Cost: $5 for members of the Association of Science-Technology Centers, $12.50 for nonmembers. Write:

> Association of Science-Technology Centers
> 2100 Pennsylvania Avenue, N.W.
> Washington, D.C. 20037

National Association of Counties (NACo)

A plethora of information for grant-seeking counties usually can be found in NACo's *County News*. For $15, you get an annual subscription to this weekly as well as the monthly supplement *New County Times* and periodic special reports. NACo also publishes a *Guide to Grantsmanship for County Official:* booklet and conducts seminars. For further information write:

>National Association of Counties
>1735 New York Avenue, N.W.
>Washington, D.C. 20006

National Center for Community Action (NCCA)

NCCA services the various community action agencies and other anti-poverty-oriented nonprofit organizations. It publishes a number of useful publications, including *Where the Money Is* and *Human Work for Human Needs,* two paperbacks that identify and briefly describe Federal government funding sources geared to help low-income people. Each book costs $5. For copies or for information on NCCA, write:

>National Center for Community Action
>1328 New York Avenue, N.W.
>Washington, D.C. 20005

National Council on Phlilanthropy (NCOP)

Though principally involved with the private fund-raising sector, NCOP's activities delve into government-grant issues. For information on the nonprofit NCOP membership organization and its well-planned conferences, write:

>National Council on Philanthropy
>680 Fifth Avenue
>New York, New York 10019

National Graduate University

Conducts seminars on government grant-seeking. Most attendees are institutional as opposed to individual grantees. Semnars take place principally in Washington, D.C., but some are also held in other cities, including Chicago, San Francisco, New Orleans, Boston, and Denver. Top seminar fee is $242. National Graduate University publishes *Grants Administration,* a book geared mainly to the needs of educational and research institutions ($6.50). For descriptive literature, write:

> National Graduate University
> 3408 Wisconsin Avenue, N.W.
> Washington, D.C. 20016

National Journal

A privately published weekly periodical containing background information on policy-shaping actions by the Executive and Legislative branches. The subscription rate is high ($300 per year), but the quality of reporting makes the *National Journal* useful to most large-scale government grant-seeking operations. Write the publisher:

> National Journal
> 1730 M Street, N.W.
> Washington, D.C. 20036

Newspapers

The best day-to-day newspaper coverage of Congressional and Executive Branch actions and plans concerning federal funding programs is in the *Washington Post.* The *New York Times* is the second-best source. Both these newspapers—particularly the *Times*—can be found in major libraries across the country.

New York University Seminars

The School of Continuing Education of New York University (SCENYU) conducts two-day seminars for federal grant-seekers in Washington, D.C. Cost: $295 tuition per person plus $50 registration fee per organization. For descriptive literature, write:

> SCENYU
> 360 Lexington Avenue
> New York, New York 10017

Oryx Press

Geared for academicians, the Oryx Press *Grant Information System* covers grants from both the public and private sectors. Grants are categorized into one hundred subject areas. Subscriptions ($375 per year plus postage) include the monthly *Faculty Alert Bulletins,* divided into six broad subject areas.

Oryx Press also researches and compiles two other publications covering public and private sector grants. The first is the hardcover *Directory of Research Grants,* which describes over seventeen hundred grants relevant to academic researchers and graduate students ($34.75 per copy). The second is the *Fund Sources in Health and Allied Fields* newsletter (annual subscription: $95).

For descriptive literature, write the publisher:

> Oryx Press
> 3930 E. Camelback Road
> Phoenix, Arizona 85018

Public Service Materials Center (PSMC)

PSMC is a private organization providing grant-seekers with a variety of books on fund raising. One, *How to Get Government Grants,* specifically relates to federal funding. If you have $13.50 to spend on a 155-page paperback, you can get this book by writing the publisher:

Public Service Materials Center
355 Lexington Avenue
New York, New York 10017

R&D Management

An excellent in-depth study of research and development
(R&D) management methods used by some of the federal agencies can be found in this 233-page hardcover book written by
three Rand Corporation scholars. For a copy, mail $15 to the
publisher:

Lexington Book Division
D.C. Heath and Company
125 Spring Street
Lexington, Massachusetts 02173

Federal Outlays

You can obtain data on the estimated annual amount of
federal-agency dollars (and other types of financial influence
such as loan guarantees) that flow into each state, county, and
25,000+-population city in a series of books: one for each
state (prices vary) and one national summary volume ($275).
This data is also available on microfiche. For details, write:

National Technical Information Service
U.S. Department of Commerce
Springfield, Virginia 22161

Soup to Nuts

A 41-page pocket-sized primer geared for grant- and contract-
seeking college personnel. Cost: $1.50. Write the publisher.

Soup to Nuts publication
Queensborough Community College
The City University of New York
Bayside, New York 11364

Smithsonian Science Information Exchange (SSIE)

SSIE, a nonprofit corporation of the Smithsonian Institution, has detailed computerized data banks on current and planned science-related research projects. This information can help you pinpoint who is funding and who is working on projects similar to yours. For literature and fee structures, write:

Smithsonian Science Information Exchange
1730 M Street, N.W.
Washington, D.C. 20036

State Central Information Reception Agencies (SCIRA)

The function of State Central Information Reception Agencies is to help ensure that state and local governments are notified of federally funded grants-in-aid that might affect their local jurisdiction. Each state has one of these reception agencies.

This information-reporting process is spelled out in TC-1082, which requires federal agencies to send to each State Central Information Reception Agency the data on the purpose and the amount of a grants-in-aid. This data is usually transmitted on the standard Federal Form 424, which must be completed and sent to the appropriate reception agency within seven days after the grant is issued.

Some reception agencies merely serve as a depository for the data, while others disseminate the data in report form to the executive and legislative officials of their respective states (and to local governmental units when applicable). In most states, the reception agencies allow the public reasonable access to the collected data.

Taft Corporation

Helping nonprofit organizations increase their fund-raising expertise through the use of modern business methods is the hallmark of the Taft Corporation, a commercial firm. The company offers consulting services as well as an array of fund-raising publications. Their services and publications are outlined in their descriptive literature, which is definitely worth requesting. Write:

> Taft Corporation
> 1000 Vermont Ave., N.W.
> Washington, D.C. 20005

Tamblyn & Brown

Tamblyn & Brown is one of the large private consulting firms serving the needs of fund-seeking organizations. For information, write:

> Tamblyn & Brown
> 1717 Massachusetts Avenue, N.W.
> Washington, D.C. 20036

United States Government Manual

The 800+-page "official handbook" of the U.S. Government is certainly worth its price because it provides you with an organized wealth of information on all federal departments, independent agencies, commissions, and quasi-governmental organizations. It describes their functions and activities, gives organization charts, lists the key personnel, and tells how and where to get additional information. The cost is $6.50 for the paperback edition. Write:

> Superintendent of Documents
> U.S. Government Printing Office
> Washington, D.C. 20402

Washington Information Directory

Well-indexed and organized, this annual 800+-page hardcover directory lists and describes the key Executive Branch, congressional, and private sources of government-related information. Entries are divided into sixteen categories, from "Communications & the Media" to "Science, Space and Transportation." The volume also provides a directory of key state officials and mayors of $50,000+-population cities. For a copy, mail $18 to:

> Washington Information Directory
> Congressional Quarterly
> 1414 22nd Street, N.W.
> Washington, D.C. 20037

Washington International Arts Letter

If your grant-seeking endeavor falls into the broad artistic spectrum, you should acquaint yourself with two publications prepared by the Washington International Arts Letter, a commercial firm.

The first is *Grants and Aid to Individuals in the Arts,* a 200+-page paperback listing and indexing grants made by foundation, corporate, and government sources. Cost: $13.95.

The second is *Washington International Arts Letter,* a ten-times-a-year newsletter. An annual subscription runs $16 for individuals, $32 for institutions.

To order the book or newsletter, or to obtain descriptive literature, write:

> Washington International Arts Letter
> 1321 4th Street, S.W.
> Washington, D.C. 20024

Weekly Compilation of Presidential Documents

Well-staffed grant-seeking organizations may consider keeping abreast of what the President is doing and planning to do by selectively reading the *Weekly Compilation of Presidential Documents*. Review copies are available at Federal Depository Libraries. Annual subscriptions run $15.00, and may be obtained by writing:

> Weekly Compilation of Presidential Documents
> Superintendent of Documents
> U.S. Government Printing Office
> Washington, D.C. 20402

Your Own Field

Collectively, the trade organizations, services, and publications within your own field offer you one of the best—if not the best—sources of grant-seeking assistance because of their sharp focus.

We have already briefly described some of these sources, such as the Center for Community Change, which specializes in helping low-income and minority community organizations. Though we would like to, it is beyond the scope and size of our book to list every specialized source, as there are over ten thousand different trade organizations and more than fifty thousand different special-interest publications serving over one thousand different fields.

Should you not already be familiar with all the trade organizations, services, and publications within your field, your best bet is to poll informally a wide cross-section of your professional colleagues. If this method is not feasible, the best general reference book for identifying trade organizations is the *Encyclopedia of Associations* (see page 168), and the best reference book for identifying special-interest publications is the *Standard Period-*

ical Directory (available at most large public and college li braries).

To illustrate how almost all the major fields have their own deep reservoir of services and publications that can help grant seekers, let's examine one—the field of education. We have already described in this chapter several education-oriented sources: Educational Funding Research Council, Oryx Press *Manual for Obtaining Government Grants* and *Soup to Nuts* But further searching will uncover other useful grant-seeking sources. For instance: *Incentive Grant Approach in Higher Education* booklet (Institute for Educational Leadership, George Washington University, 1001 Connecticut Avenue, N.W. Washington, D.C. 20036); National Council of University Re search Administrators membership organization (NCURA 4416 Edmunds Street, N.W., Washington, D.C. 20007); *Educa tional Resources Newsletter* (Educational Resource Systems 1200 Pennsylvania Avenue, N.W., Washington, D.C. 20044) "Guide to Federal Assistance for Education" $375-per-year information service (New Century Education Corporation, 440 Park Avenue South, New York, New York 10016); "College and University Reporter" $625 per year information service (Commerce Clearinghouse, 4025 West Peterson, Chicago, Illi nois 60646); College Resource Development Service (Cassell and Associates, 104 South Michigan Avenue, Chicago, Illinois 60603); *Chronicle of Higher Education* weekly (1717 Massa chusetts Avenue, N.W., Washington, D.C. 20036); *American Education* magazine (U.S. Office of Education, 400 Maryland Avenue, S.W., Washington, D.C. 20202); *Higher Education and National Affairs* publication (American Council on Edu cation, 1 Dupont Circle, N.W., Washington, D.C. 20036) *Educational Researcher* (American Education Research As sociation, 1216 Sixteenth Street, N.W., Washington, D.C. 20036).

The degree of grant-seeking usefulness of the various trade organizations, services, and publications within your field will, of course, range from barren to fertile. It will take a little investigatory work on your part to determine their value to your own grant-seeking needs—but that effort usually pays good down-the-road dividends.

Other Publications Discussed in Part Two

You will also find other publications listed under the various funding agencies described in Part II, "Where the Money Is." Most of those publications are too specialized for general use. However, five of them offer such broad tips and insights that they should become part of every grant-seeker's basic library: three Public Health Service publications (page 71), *How to Do Business with DHEW* (page 74) and *Grants for Scientific Research* (page 108).

APPENDIXES

APPENDIX A

History and Trends

History in Brief

Government financial assistance can be traced back to prehistoric times when small primitive villages built community irrigation systems. But federal financial assistance as we know it today is a relatively recent phenomenon that was ushered in during the days of President Franklin D. Roosevelt's New Deal in the early 1930s. Even by those standards, FDR's financial-aid programs were minuscule compared to what we have today. To illustrate, in Fiscal Year 1935 the Roosevelt administration spent $3 billion on social welfare. Just forty years later, in Fiscal Year 1975, the figure rose to $166 billion.

Numerous funding programs have been enacted by Congress since the start of the Roosevelt era. This legislation includes:

> Home Loan Act—1933
> Social Security Act—1935
> FICA Act—1938
> G.I. Bill—1944
> National Science Foundation Act—1950
> National Defense Education Act—1958
> Vocational Rehabilitation Act—1963
> Higher Education Act—1965
> National Endowment on the Arts
> and the Humanities Act—1965
> General Revenue Sharing—1972

Trends in Brief

The key recent trend is the New Federalism philosophy. Under it, some of the decision-making power on how government funds should be spent is being transferred from Washington to state and local levels. Outgrowths of New Federalism include the A-95 Clearinghouse Review Process and General Revenue Sharing.

Another trend is a more open dissemination of government information to grant-seekers. This is guaranteed under the Freedom of Information Act (see page 118).

Still another major trend is Zero-Based Budgeting (President Carter's version) and Sunset (Congress's version). The principal purpose of both these systems is to weed out obsolete funding programs. Under these systems, all but a few funding programs must be reapproved by a positive action on the part of Congress and the President at least every five years (or so) or the programs automatically become extinct. This prevents a funding program from remaining on the books well beyond its usefulness simply because Congress doesn't want to take the step of voting it off the books because of fear of political repercussions from benefiting special interest groups.

No one knows for sure what the future holds—at least not in terms of government grants. A change of administration, for instance, can alter the amount and focus of government funding. But whatever political philosophy reigns in the White House, it seems reasonably certain that the trend toward New Federalism and its attendant geographical decentralization of grant-making decisions will continue. The growth of increased government grant funding will also probably continue, at least in the foreseeable future. Government grants are here to stay, whether we politically are in favor of them or not.

New agencies will come into existence while old ones will die or merge. New funding programs will be brought forth by Congress and the President in reaction to changing public needs and demands—and to unforeseen developments (such as the financial collapse of New York City or an urban renewal program in response to widespread ghetto unrest).

While there will be increased government funding, the competition for these dollars will be even keener. Consequently, grant-seekers will have to be more sophisticated tomorrow than today in their funding quests if they are to be successful.

APPENDIX B

Grant Genesis

If you are a medium- to large-scale government grant-seeker, it will probably pay you to follow grant programs from their genesis. There are two major reasons for our suggestion: you will be gaining extra lead time by knowing what's coming down the government grant-making pipeline and you'll have a chance to give your views when the proposed legislation is still being debated by the House and Senate committees and subcommittees (see Step 5 below).

This Appendix gives you a thumbnail sketch of the path taken by a typical proposed bill—but keep in mind that other routes are possible. (For instance, a congressman may propose a bill on his own initiative.)

STEP 1: The President decides that the country needs a new funding program.

STEP 2: The President enlists a congressman to sponsor the proposed bill in the House of Representatives. (The President also enlists a senator to sponsor the proposed bill in the Senate. This legislative body will deal with the proposed bill using procedures almost identical with those outlined for the House of Representatives in Steps 3 to 7.)

STEP 3: The congressional sponsor introduces the proposed legislation on the floor of the House of Representatives.

STEP 4: The sponsor's proposed bill is assigned to the appropriate committee(s). This committee may in turn assign the proposed bill to one or more of its subcommittees.

STEP 5: The sponsor's proposed bill is studied and revised first by the subcommittee (if one is involved) and then by the committee. It is during this stage of the legislative process that you, as a concerned citizen or organization, can most effectively voice your opinions—either in person or by letter, telegram, or telephone.

STEP 6: Three possibilities exist on the committee (and subcommittee) level. First, the committee's version of the proposed bill is voted down, in which case the proposed bill either dies or is revised (for reconsideration). Second, the proposed bill is "tabled indefinitely." (This is tantamount to its being killed.) Third, the proposed bill is passed either in its original form or with revisions and/or amendments.

STEP 7: If the committee passes the proposed bill, it is sent to the floor of the House of Representatives for a vote by its full membership. The House can either pass it (a majority vote is required) or vote it down and return it to the committee for possible further revision. In the latter case, the step 4 to 7 cycle begins anew.

STEP 8: If by this time both the Senate and the House of Representatives have passed the proposed bill, some of their senior members get together for a "conference" meeting. This meeting is essential because in almost every instance the House and Senate versions of the proposed bill will be somewhat different. The conference committee members negotiate and resolve their differences in order to come up with a compromise proposed bill that will be suitable to both the House and Senate. This compromise proposed bill is then returned to the House and Senate for a majority-vote approval.

STEP 9: If both the House and Senate approve (by majority vote) the conference committee's compromise proposed bill, it is sent to the President for signature. If either the House or Senate does not approve the conference committee's compromise proposed bill, it is returned to the conference committee for further negotiation and revision until a mutually satisfactory proposed bill emerges.

STEP 10: If the bill is jointly passed by both the House and Senate, the President has two options. First, he can sign the proposed bill, in which case it immediately becomes law. Second, he can veto the proposed bill. In this instance, Congress can do one of three things: give up the proposed bill as a lost cause; revise it and send it back to the President; override the President's veto. This last action requires a two-thirds vote in both chambers.

STEP 11: A funding program bill may be passed and *authorized,* but until the House of Representatives *appropriates* the money, no Treasury dollars will be available to the funding agency.

STEP 12: Once the money is appropriated, the funding agency can start making grants.

After the law is enacted, the Executive Branch agency draws up formal regulations (eligibility requirements, review criteria, et cetera) to govern the program. These regulations, should—but do not always—reflect congressional intent. They are published in the *Federal Register.*

Another important facet of the government funding system with which you should be familiar is the rescission and deferral process. A rescission occurs when the President eliminates all or part of the funds appropriated for a program. To go into effect, the rescission must be approved by both the House and Senate within forty-five days after the President requests it. A deferral occurs when the President wishes to delay spending all or some of the appropriated funds for a program. This deferral cannot extend beyond the current fiscal year. Either the House or Senate can override the President's deferral, providing one of them does so within sixty days after the President requests the deferral. If neither chamber acts within this time period, the deferral becomes official. For a list of the rescissions and deferrals requested by the President, check the *Federal Register,* as the Chief Executive must by law publish this information each month in that government periodical. For details on the law governing the rescission and deferral process, read the Congressional Budget and Impoundment Control Act of 1974.

APPENDIX C

The Bureaucratic Monster

"Bureaucracy"—that's a word that raises the hackles of most citizens. But does government bureaucracy really exist or is it merely a convenient label to pin on an organizational system that doesn't work as quickly and smoothly as we might wish?

We asked a number of people whether they thought bureaucracy exists and received "yes," "no" and "maybe" answers, depending on whom we asked. We personally belong to the camp that believes that a bureaucratic monster is alive and well and living in Washington, D.C. Some of this demon's pet tricks and stratagems are:

The Monster loves paperwork. It has been estimated by the Commission on Federal Paperwork (such a body really exists) that paperwork and red tape cost our country's economy a whopping $40 billion a year. To help prove its point, the Commission in a public meeting unrolled a 45-foot-long string of forms, the paperwork to process a single child through the Aid to Dependent Children program. The Commission also illustrated its case against excess paperwork by telling of a single project that generated enough paperwork to keep up to forty individuals busy for four years.

The Monster knows that if your request sits on top of its desk long enough, the problem may resolve itself through time—or perhaps you may forget or give up on your request. Either way, the Monster has saved time and effort.

If the Monster doesn't have the time to deal with you, it may temporarily or permanently get you off its back by shuttling you off to another government employee, whether or not that employee can help you. This is one of the reasons why you often get ping-ponged between government officials.

Unless you specifically know and request what you want, the Monster won't give it to you, even if the Monster knows you are in need of it. In short, while the Monster may (if you are fortunate) do exactly and precisely what you request, it will do little more.

If the material you request is temporarily unavailable, the Monster will purposely send you unrelated material. This tactic allows the Monster to toss your request letter into the circular file rather than being forced to keep it in the "to do later" file.

The Monster minimizes its risk by taking no action rather than taking a positive step.

If the Monster can misunderstand your request, your request will be misunderstood (a variation of Murphy's Law).

On the other hand, we could make a similar and perhaps longer list of examples of how we—the public—irritate government officials with our actions. But rather than insulting ourselves with the facts, we'll let the matter rest . . . .

APPENDIX D

A-95 Clearinghouse Review Process

Of the many Federal-government-grant decision-making processes, the A-95 Clearinghouse Review System is one of the most baffling ones to neophyte grant-seekers. To help you gain perspective, we have prepared this Appendix, which describes the process in broad brushstrokes.

The "A-95" Name

The "A-95 Clearinghouse Review System" name derives from the OMB Circular A-95, which defines and lays down the rules for the review process.

Purpose

The underlying purpose of the A-95 Clearinghouse Review System is straightforward. It seeks to prevent the Federal government from funding projects that might duplicate or conflict with the plans and programs of subnational units (including state and local governments, regional boards, and public agencies). A look back into the past will help substantiate the need for the A-95 review system. There have been instances, for example, where HUD has funded a housing development project in neighborhood A, while the community planning board would have preferred to have had the project in neighborhood B.

The Scope

Of the many federal assistance programs, some two hundred are subject to the A-95 review process. General program areas that usually fall within the A-95 domain include economic and regional development, urban renewal and housing, community health, education, law enforcement, the aging, and other types of funding that have direct state, regional, or local impact. Even the construction of a federal highway or a veterans' hospital requires the A-95 review process.

Does Your Project Require the A-95 Review Process?

If you want to determine if your funding program requires the A-95 review process, the quickest, most authoritative source is the funding program officer. Other reliable sources include the Office of Management and Budget (which administers the A-95 program) and the regional A-95 coordinators (based out of the ten Federal Regional Councils). *The Catalog of Federal Domestic Assistance* is also a good source, but the information can sometimes be out of date.

The Clearinghouses

There are two basic types of clearinghouses: state and area-wide. If your project is subject to the A-95 review process, it must be reviewed by both these clearinghouses, which are subnational governmental committee-type bodies. Their function is to ascertain whether your project is consistent with the other plans and programs within their respective geographic area. Their "yes" or "no" evaluation is passed along to the federal funding agency from which you are seeking the grant.

Project Notification and Review System (PNRS)

In complying with the A-95 review process, you must follow certain steps that are collectively known as the Project Notification and Review System. Here is a condensed summary of the PNRS system:

STEP 1: Determine if the federal funding program from which you are seeking a grant is subject to the A-95 review process. If the answer is "no," you need no longer be concerned with the A-95 review process (unless your state laws say otherwise). If the answer is "yes," you must notify both the appropriate state and areawide clearinghouses of your intent to seek the federal funds. Your communication is referred to as the NOI or "Notification of Intent." Your NOI must be accompanied by a summary of your proposed project.

STEP 2: Your NOI is examined by each clearinghouse—and by other jurisdictional governmental bodies and public agencies should the clearinghouse feel that the impact of your project might affect those entities. The clearinghouse has but thirty days to complete this review process. Three possibilities exist:

No issues are raised about your project. In such a case, the clearinghouse "signs off" your NOI. This "signing off" procedure assures the federal funding agency that your project does not run counter to any of the plans and programs within the clearinghouse's geographic area.

Issues are raised by either the clearinghouse or the outside jurisdictional bodies and public service agencies. If this happens, the clearinghouse officially notifies you of this fact —and you proceed to Step 3.

The clearinghouse gives you no decision within thirty days after you have submitted your NOI. If this is the situation, you have the right to interpret this nonaction as "signing off." When submitting your final application to the federal agency, you simply make note of the lack of concrete action on the part of the clearinghouse. However, should the thirty-day deadline expire, the clearinghouse can still give its opinions to the funding agency. In this case, the clearinghouse submits its opinions directly to the funding agency instead of having its opinions piggyback on your completed application that you will be submitting to the agency.

STEP 3: If issues are raised during Step 2, the clearinghouse usually tries to get you and your critic(s) together to negotiate and resolve your differences. If these differences are resolved, the clearinghouse "signs off." If the differences are not resolved, you must give the clearinghouse your completed application so that the objector has an opportunity to scrutinize it. This critic then submits to the clearinghouse the objections—in writing. The clearinghouse returns to you your completed application (which must be within thirty days after you've submitted it) along with the written objections from the clearinghouse itself and/or from the outside critic.

STEP 4: You submit to the federal agency your completed application along with the written objections. If you like, you may submit written rebuttals to those objections.

STEP 5: The federal agency reviews your completed application. Concurrently, it takes into consideration the written objections, though it doesn't have any legal obligation to heed them. A clearinghouse, in other words, has only advisory power. But that power is usually quite influential, as numerous case histories have shown.

Further Information

The Office of Management and Budget (OMB) has two very informative publications on the A-95 review process. Both are available free by writing:

> Intergovernmental Relations and
> Regional Operations Division
> Office of Management and Budget
> New Executive Office Building
> Washington, D.C. 20503

A-95: WHAT IT IS—HOW IT WORKS—A forty-page handbook explaining the A-95 review process in layman's language.

CIRCULAR A-95 AND ATTACHMENTS—A stapled fifty-page document detailing the A-95 review process in legal language.

APPENDIX E

Student Aid

*If you are a student seeking government financial aid, you
will find many sound pointers throughout this book. To
help you further, we've prepared this Appendix.*

Several million students will receive billions of dollars in government financial aid this year. We estimate that at least a million more students could receive federal funds if they knew they were eligible and if they understood the application procedures

Basic Educational Opportunity Grants (BEOG)

The principal type of federal aid to students is a program entitled Basic Educational Opportunity Grants. These grants are available to full-time, or at least half-time, undergraduate students who have been accepted by one of the over five thousand colleges, vocational, technical, or career training schools accredited by the Basic Grant Program. To be eligible, the student must verify his or her need for financial assistance. This need is based upon the student's and his or her family's financial well-being. Grants can range from $50 to about $1,000 per academic year. These funds are outright grants and do not have to be repaid.

To help you determine whether—and to what degree—you are eligible, the U.S. Office of Education has prepared its *Eligibility Index* pamphlet. For a free copy of it and the Basic Grant application form, write:

Basic Grants
U.S. Office of Education
Department of Health, Education, and Welfare
Washington, D.C. 20202

National Direct Student Loan (NDSL)

While the Basic Opportunity Grant is the principal type of federal aid giving money to students, the National Direct Student Loan is the principal lending program. This federally funded and usually college-administered program offers low (currently 3 percent) interest loans directly to students in need of assistance. When accepting a National Direct Student Loan, you must realize that you are signing a binding contract and are legally responsible to repay the debt. Although this money must be repaid, the student is given a nine-month grace period upon graduation before the first payment is due. Extensions are given to those who will be continuing their academic education on a graduate level, or, in exceptional cases, where the student is severely depressed financially. (Some students have been known to rip off the system by declaring personal bankruptcy, or by being negligent in paying back their loans. While this may temporarily get them off the hook, it can seriously affect their lifelong credit rating.)

Other Major Types of Federal Assistance

Supplemental Educational Opportunity Grants: This program awards money to students whose need for financial assistance is exceptional. Grants in this program range from about $200 to $1,500 per academic year. For further information, contact the U.S. Office of Education (address above).

Student Loans: The Federal government insures student loans, thereby enabling commercial lending institutions (such as banks, insurance companies, et cetera) to lend students money at a comparatively low interest rate. For specific details or general

information on this type of loan, contact the appropriate lendin
institution or write:

> Bureau of Higher Education
> U.S. Office of Higher Education
> Washington, D.C. 20202.

Federally insured student loans from other funding source
are available to full-time students who meet specific criteria
such as preparing for a career in nursing, scientific research, o
the health profession.

College Work Study Program: Under this program student
can supplement their incomes by working on partially sub
sidized part-time jobs either on or off campus. Though hourl
wages are the same for all students, the number of hours a
student is permitted to work varies according to need. Elig:bl
participants earn from $400 to $2,500 annually. Urban Corp
(which is a separate agency supervised by the mayor's office i
many cities) cooperates with the College Work Study Progran
to help find partially subsidized part-time employment for stu
dents. The off-campus positions provided by Urban Corps are
with nonprofit organizations such as day-care centers, the
YMCA, or the Jewish Guild for the Blind.

Cooperative Education Program (CEP): Under the CEF
program, a student works full time on a government job for one
semester, then alternates the following semester with concen
trated full-time study. For information on eligibility require
ments and application procedures, contact your regional Civi
Service Commission office.

G.I. Bill: Congress has enacted special legislation giving stu
dent aid to Vietnam War veterans. Benefits run a little over
$300 per month for full-time single veterans, slightly more for
veterans with dependents. Widows (and, in some cases, chil
dren) of Vietnam War servicemen are also eligible under the
same legislation. Up until their twenty-third birthday, children
of deceased or disabled Korean War servicemen can also re-

eive student-aid benefits. For details, contact your local veterans' office or write:

Veterans Administration
810 Vermont Avenue N.W.
Washington, D.C. 20420

Apprenticeship Programs: The Federal government sponsors a broad range of apprentice programs for students entering into positions requiring a skill or craft. Examples of apprenticeship programs include carpentry, silversmithing, plumbing, and pipe-fitting.

State Programs

Most states have some form of student financial aid for their residents. The requirements for the available dollars varies from state to state and program to program within a state. In most cases, funds are awarded according to need and/or scholastic achievement. For specific information, contact your State Department of Education.

Sources of Information

Your best information source on government (and other) student-aid programs is, in most cases, your school's financial-aid office. This is true because student-aid programs are forever changing—new ones are created and old ones dry up. The staff of the student-aid offices are usually up to date on what is current and forthcoming. They can also answer many of your questions on the spot.

The major published sources include the *Annual Register of Grant Support* (see page 156), *Grants Register* (see page 178), and the *Guide to Financial Aid for Students and Parents.* The last book (as well as a number of other student-aid publications) is for sale at most bookstores located on or near campuses.

APPENDIX F

Forms of Address

Protocol suggests the use of certain forms of address and salutations when corresponding with high-ranking government personnel. While there are other perfectly proper alternatives, the following are the ones most widely accepted as being socially and officially correct.

THE PRESIDENT OF THE UNITED STATES:

The President
The White House
Washington, D.C.   20500

My dear Mr. President:

THE VICE PRESIDENT OF THE UNITED STATES:

The Vice President
Washington, D.C.   20510

My dear Mr. Vice President:

CABINET MEMBERS:

The Honorable John Doe
The Secretary of State
Washington, D.C.   20520

My dear Mr. Secretary:

or

The Honorable John Doe
The Attorney General
Washington, D.C.   20530

My dear Mr. Attorney General:

NDERSECRETARIES AND DEPUTY SECRETARIES OF EXECUTIVE DEPARTMENTS:

The Honorable John Doe
Under Secretary of Commerce
Washington, D.C.   20230

My dear Mr. Secretary:

or

The Honorable John Doe
Deputy Secretary of Labor
Washington, D.C.   20210

My dear Mr. Secretary:

SSISTANT SECRETARIES OF EXECUTIVE DEPART-MENTS:

The Honorable John Doe
Assistant Secretary of Transportation
Washington, D.C.   20590

My dear Mr. Doe:

OMMISSIONER, CHAIRMAN, DIRECTOR, OR CHIEF OF A GOVERNMENT OFFICE:

The Honorable John Doe, Chairman
Equal Employment Opportunity Commission
Washington, D.C.   20506

My dear Mr. Chairman:

HE PRESIDENT OF THE SENATE

The President of the Senate
United States Senate
Washington, D.C.   20510

My dear Mr. Vice President:

UNITED STATES SENATORS:

The Honorable John Doe
United States Senate
Washington, D.C.   20510

to a home-state address:
The Honorable John Doe
United States Senator
Federal Building
85 Marconi Avenue
Columbus, Ohio   43215

My dear Senator Doe:

THE SPEAKER OF THE UNITED STATES HOUSE OF REPRESENTATIVES:

The Honorable John Doe
The Speaker of the House of Representatives
Washington, D.C.   20515

My dear Mr. Speaker:

UNITED STATES CONGRESSMEN:

The Honorable John Doe
United States House of Representatives
Washington, D.C.   20515

to a home-state address:
The Honorable John Doe
Representative, U.S. Congress
Post Office Building
301 Chickamauga Avenue
Rossville, Georgia   30741

My dear Mr. Doe:

APPENDIX G

Acronyms

Washington loves to use acronyms and abbreviations. Here is a list of the ones you are most likely to encounter on your grant quest.

AACC	Adjustment Assistance Coordinating Committee
ABC	American Biological Council
ACDA	Arms Control and Disarmament Agency
ACE	Active Corps of Executives
ACIR	Advisory Commission on Intergovernmental Relations
ACP	Agricultural Conservation Program
ACV	ACTION Cooperative Volunteer Program
ADAP	Airport Development Aid Program
ADP	Automatic Data Processing
A/E	Architectural/Engineering
AFDC	Aid to Families with Dependent Children
AIC	Apprenticeship Information Center
AID	Agency for International Development
AMS	Agricultural Marketing Service
AOP	Apprenticeship Outreach Program
APC	Air Pollution Control
APHIS	Animal and Plant Health Inspection Service
APTD	Aid to the Permanently and Totally Disabled
ARC	American Red Cross
ARC	Appalachian Regional Commission
ARS	Agricultural Research Service
ASCS	Agricultural Stabilization and Conservation Service
ASEE	American Society for Engineering Education
ASPR	Armed Services Procurement Regulation
ASTI	Applied Statistics Training Institute
AVIE	Adult, Vocational, and Technical Education
BAVTE	Bureau of Adult, Vocational, and Technical Education
BEH	Bureau of Education for the Handicapped
BEPD	Bureau of Educational Personnel Development
BIA	Bureau of Indian Affairs
BLM	Bureau of Land Management
BLS	Bureau of Labor Statistics
BOR	Bureau of Outdoor Recreation

CAB	Civil Aeronautics Board
CBO	Community Based Organizations
CBO	Congressional Budget Office
CCI	Course Content Improvement
CCSS	Cooperative College School Service
CDA	City Demonstration Agency
CDS	Construction Differential Subsidies
CFDA	Catalog of Federal Domestic Assistance
CFTC	Commodity Futures Trading Commission
CFN	Community Food and Nutrition
CFR	Code of Federal Regulations
CMHC	Community Mental Health Centers
CHP	Comprehensive Health Planning
CHS	Community Health Service
CLEO	Council on Legal Education Opportunity
CPI	Consumer Price Index
CPRC	Coastal Plains Regional Commission
CRS	Community Relations Service
CSA	Community Services Administration
CSC	Civil Service Commission
CSRS	Cooperative State Research Service
DBL	Displaced Business Loans
DCPA	Defense Civil Preparedness Agency
DEA	Drug Enforcement Administration
DIBA	Domestic and International Business Administration
DOD	Department of Defense
DOT	Department of Transportation
DSA	Defense Supply Agency
ECM	Emergency Conservation Measures
EEOC	Equal Employment Opportunity Commission
EIDL	Economic Injury Disaster Loans
EMI	Exchange of Medical Information
EMS	Emergency Medical Services
EMS	Export Marketing Service
EO	Executive Order
EOC	Emergency Operating Centers
EOL	Economic Opportunity Loans
EPA	Environmental Protection Agency
EPDA	Education Professions Development Act
ERDA	Energy Research and Development Administration
ERS	Economic Research Service
ES	Employment Service
ESA	Employment Standards Administration
ESEA	Elementary and Secondary Education Act
FAA	Federal Aviation Administration
FAIR	Fair Access to Insurance Requirements
FAS	Foreign Agricultural Service
FBI	Federal Bureau of Investigation
FCC	Federal Communications Commission
FCRC	Four Corners Regional Commission

CS   Farmer Cooperative Service
DA   Food and Drug Administration
DAA   Federal Disaster Assistance Administration
HA   Federal Housing Administration
mHA   Farmers Home Administration
HWA   Federal Highway Administration
IA   Federal Insurance Administration
IP   Forestry Incentives Program
MC   Federal Management Circular
MC   Federal Maritime Commission
MCS   Federal Mediation and Conciliation Service
NMA   Federal National Mortgage Association ('Fannie Mae')
NS   Food and Nutrition Service
PMS   Flood Plain Management Services
R   Federal Register
R   Funding Request
RA   Federal Railroad Administration
SS   Federal Supply Service
TC   Federal Trade Commission
Y   Fiscal Year

AO   General Accounting Office
ARP   Global Atmosphere Research Program
FA   General Forestry Assistance
NP   Gross National Product
PO   Government Printing Office
RS   General Revenue Sharing
SA   General Services Administration

AL   Handicapped Assistance Loans
EW   Department of Health, Education, and Welfare
G   Housing Guaranty
IP   Hospital Improvement
IST   Hospital In-Service Training
MO   Health Maintenance Organization
PSL   Health Professions Student Loans
SA   Health Systems Agencies
SGT   High Speed Ground Transportation
UD   Department of Housing and Urban Development

CC   Interstate Commerce Commission
DOE   International Decade of Ocean Exploration
NS   Immigration and Naturalization Service
PA   Intergovernmental Personnel Act
REX   International Research and Exchange Board
RS   International Revenue Service

SIP   Job Service Improvement Program

DD   Local Development District
EA   Local Educational Agency
EAA   Law Enforcement Assistance Administration
EAP   Laboratory Evaluation and Accreditation Program
EEP   Law Enforcement Education Program
MSA   Labor-Management Services Administration

MA	Maritime Administration
MARC	Minority Access to Research Careers
MBOC	Minority Business Opportunity Committee
MCA	Model Cities Administration
MCH	Maternal and Child Health
MDTA	Manpower Development and Training Act
MEDLARS	Medical Literature Analysis and Retrieval Systems
MESA	Mining Enforcement and Safety Administration
MVP	Minority Vendors Program
MESBIC	Minority Enterprise Small Business Investment Company
NAB	National Alliance of Businessmen
NADIS	National Aerometric Data Information System
NARA	Narcotic Addict Rehabilitation Act
NASA	National Aeronautics and Space Administration
NATO	North Atlantic Treaty Organization
NBS	National Bureau of Standards
NCAA	National Collegiate Athletic Association
NCHSRD	National Center for Health Services Research and Development
NCIC	National Crime Information Center
NCJISS	National Criminal Justice Information and Statistic Service
NCSBCS	National Conference of States on Building Codes an Standards
NCUA	National Credit Union Administration
NDEA	National Defense Education Act
NDSL	National Defense Student Loan
NEA	National Education Association
NEA	National Endowment for the Arts
NEDS	National Emission Data Systems
NEH	National Endowment for the Humanities
NEI	National Eye Institute
NEPA	National Environmental Policy Act
NERC	New England Regional Commission
NESA	National Environmenal Study Areas
NHTSA	National Highway Transportation Safety Administration
NIAID	National Institute of Allergy and Infectious
NIDA	National Institute on Drug Abuse Diseases
NIDR	National Institute of Dental Research
NIE	National Institute of Education
NIEHS	National Institute of Environmental Health Sciences
NIGMS	National Institute of General Medical Services
NIH	National Institutes of Health
NIMH	National Institute of Mental Health
NINDS	National Institute of Neurological Diseases and Strok
NLM	National Library of Medicine
NLRB	National Labor Relations Board
NMFS	National Marine Fisheries Service
NOAA	National Oceanic and Atmospheric Administration
NPS	National Park Service

NRC	Nuclear Regulatory Commission
NRSA	National Research Service Awards
NSF	National Science Foundation
NSRDS	National Standard Reference Data System
NSVP	National Student Volunteer Program
NSYSP	National Summer Youth Sports Program
NTIS	National Technical Information Service
NWS	National Weather Service
OAWP	Office of Air and Water Programs
OBD	Office of Business Development
OCD	Office of Child Development
ODS	Operating Differential Subsidy
OE	Office of Education
OEDP	Overall Economic Development Program
OEMA	Office of Educational and Manpower Assistance
OFCCP	Office of Federal Contract Compliance Programs
OHD	Office of Human Development
OHI	Office for Handicapped Individuals
OJT	On-the-Job Training
OLEP	Office of Law Enforcement Programs
OMB	Office of Management and Budget
OMBE	Office of Minority Business Enterprise
OME	Office of Minerals Exploration
OPIC	Overseas Private Investment Corporation
ORC	Ozarks Regional Commission
ORS	Office of Revenue Sharing
OSH	Occupational Safety and Health
OWHM	Office of Water and Hazardous Materials
OWRC	Old West Regional Commission
OWRT	Office of Water Research and Technology
PACE	Projects to Advance Creativity in Education
PCPFS	President's Council on Physical Fitness and Sports
PDL	Product Disaster Loans
PGP	Planning Grant Program
PHA	Public Housing Authority
PHS	Public Health Service
PNRC	Pacific Northwest Regional Commission
PPBS	Planning-Programming-Budgeting System
PUR	Program of University Research
PWEDA	Public Works and Economic Development Act
RANN	Research Applied to National Needs
RCDA	Research Career Development Awards
R&D	Research and Development
RD&D	Research Development and Demonstration
REA	Rural Electrification Administration
RFP	Request for Proposals
RHD	Rural Housing Disaster
RMA	Research and Marketing Act
RMA	Regional Manpower Administration
RMP	Regional Medical Program
RMS	Rural Manpower Service

RRB	Railroad Retirement Board
RSA	Rehabilitation Services Administration
RSVP	Retired Senior Volunteer Program
SBA	Small Business Administration
SBIC	Small Business Investment Company
SCIRA	State Central Information Reception Agency
SCMR	Secretary's Committee on Mental Retardation
SCORE	Service Corps of Retired Executives
SCS	Soil Conservation Service
SEC	Securities and Exchange Commission
SEOG	Supplementary Educational Opportunity Grants
SEP	Student Expense Program
SF	Standard Form
SOS	Senior Opportunities and Services
SSI	Supplementary Security Income
SSIE	Smithsonian Science Information Exchange
SITES	Smithsonian Institution Traveling Exhibition Service
SLCD	Surplus Land for Community Development
SMC	Soil and Moisture Conservation
SMSA	Standard Metropolitan Statistical Area
SPU	School Personnel Utilization
SRM	Standard Reference Materials
SRS	Social and Rehabilitation Service
SRS	Statistical Reporting Service
SSA	Social Security Administration
STORET	Storage and Retrieval System
STRI	Smithsonian Tropical Research Institute
TAA	Trade Adjustment Assistance
TC	Treasury Circular
TEAM	Training in Expanded Auxiliary Management
TIA	Teacher Investigator Awards
TTC	Transportation Test Center
TU	Technology Utilization
TVA	Tennessee Valley Authority
UGLRC	Upper Great Lakes Regional Commission
UMIA	Urban Mass Transportation Administration
UNESCO	United Nations Educational, Scientific and Cultural O ganization
UNICEF	United Nations International Children's Emergenc Fund
URT	University Research and Training
USA	United States Army
USAF	United States Air Force
USC	United States Code
USCG	United States Coast Guard
USDA	United States Department of Agriculture
USIA	United States Information Agency
USIS	United States Information Service
USMC	United States Marine Corp
USN	United States Navy

USTC	United States Tariff Commission
USTES	United States Training and Employment Service
USTS	United States Travel Service
UYA	University Year for Action
VA	Veterans Administration
VER	Veterans Employment Representatives
VES	Veterans Employment Services
VISTA	Volunteers in Service to America
VRA	Vocational Rehabilitation Act
WAC	Women's Army Corp
WAVES	Women Accepted for Volunteer Emergency Service
WHO	World Health Organization
WIC	Women, Infants and Children Programs
WIN	Work Incentives Program
WPC	Water Pollution Control
WPI	Wholesale Price Index
WQO	Water Quality Office
WRC	Water Resources Council
WRSIC	Water Resources Scientific Information Center
YCP	Youth Challenge Program
YOC	Youth Opportunity Center

APPENDIX H

Types of Grants

Below are the key terms used to describe the various mechanisms used by the Federal government to channel grants and other forms of domestic assistance to the nation. Many of these terms as you will note, overlap.

Block Grant: Refers to grants in which the Federal government merely stipulates in broad terms how the state and local governments should spend federal aid. The tactical decision on where the money should be spent is left to the discretion of state and local officials. The purpose of block grants is to decentralize federal decision-making power. In some circles, block grants are referred to as "bloc" grants.

Capitation Grant: A formula grant (see) based on a head count such as school enrollment.

Categorical Grant: A more restrictive version of the block grant (see above), as the categorical grant spells out in greater detail the specific categories in which the money must be spent. For instance: Lunch programs for the aged.

Conference Grant: Money used to underwrite all or part of the costs of meetings, seminars, et cetera.

Consortium Grant: Federal funds funneled to one organization that will in turn share the money with other organizations jointly working on a project.

Construction Grant: Funds to be used for building, expanding, or modernizing facilities.

Continuing Education Grant: Funds used to further or to update the training of an individual (whose future services are deemed critical to the well-being of the country by the Federal govenment).

Continuing Research Grant: Designed to simplify the renewal proc-

ess of the standard research grant and to give the recipient of
such a grant a semiassurance that it will be renewed beyond the
first year.

Contract: See *Government Grant vs. Contract* below.

Corporate Grant: Philanthropic money awarded by a commercial
enterprise rather than by a foundation or a government. A
corporate grant is not to be confused with a corporate foundation
grant, in which case the money comes from a foundation established and funded by the corporation. (*The Art of Winning Corporate Grants* will be one of our forthcoming books.)

Cost Sharing: See *Matching Funds*

Demonstration Grant: Funds used to underwrite a feasibility study.
For instance: to test the assumption that a new drug-rehabilitation
program actually works.

Discretionary Grant: Exists when the federal grant administrator has
the decision-making authority to select the project, grantee,
and/or grant amount. This type of grant is in direct contrast with
a formula grant (see) where the grant administrator has minimal
decision-making influence.

Entitlement Grant: This type of grant assures that the applicant will
receive the money as long as the necessary criteria are met.
Grant-seekers are not competing for the same dollars—everyone
who is eligible will receive them. Examples of entitlement grants
include food stamps and benefits to veterans.

Excess and Surplus Property: "Excess property" consists of assets
no longer needed by a particular federal agency. Here is how the
system works: First, the agency with the excess property notifies
the General Services Administration, which in turn asks other
federal agencies whether they (or their grantees or contractors)
can use the assets. If the answer is "yes," GSA transfers the goods
along with the title to them. If the answer is "no," the assets become "surplus property," which the GSA can donate to subnational governmental units and nonprofit organizations. Or the
GSA can sell the surplus property to a private party.

Fellowship: A grant awarded to an individual to further his or her
level of professional competence. For instance: a post-doctoral
fellowship.

Flow-Through Money: Funds that go through the hands of a middle-
man. For instance, certain federal funds for primary and sec-

ondary education are "passed through" the state governments on their way to the local school boards. Another example of "flow-through" money is a consortium grant (see).

ica's twenty-five thousand private grant-giving foundations.

Formula Grant: Awarded by federal agencies on the basis of a set formula such as so many dollars for population, per capita income, enrollment, et cetera. Chief recipients: state governments. (Compare with *Discretionary Grant.*)

Foundation Grant: Philanthropic money awarded by one of America's twenty-five thousand private grant-giving foundations.

General Revenue Sharing: See page 95.

Gifts-In-Kind: A contribution or payment made in lieu of cash. Donated equipment and services are examples.

Government Grant: In the day-to-day conversation of most people, this term connotes a grant made by the Federal government. However, state (and to a lesser extent, local) governmental units also make grants.

Government Grant vs. Contract: There is sometimes a hazy line between a government grant and a government contract. In broad terms, a grant is awarded to serve the general well-being of the public (such as money to finance a drug-rehabilitation center). A government contract is awarded to secure the goods and services the government needs to carry out its various functions (such as military equipment for the navy, pencils for the Treasury Department's accounting office, and pest control advice for the Department of Agriculture).

Grants-In-Aid: Generally refers to federal grants given directly to state and local governments.

Matching Funds: Money that must be matched with a predetermined amount of funds or gifts-in-kind coming from another public or private source. If the required matching funds must come from the grantee, the process is referred to as "cost-sharing."

Planning Grant: Funds that are used to pay the costs of designing and developing a program or activity.

Project Grant: An over-all term for the wide variety of grants (such as a research grant) that supports a specific project. Normally, the recipient is not liable if the funded endeavor fails.

Purchase of Service (*POS*): When the government wants certain services rendered to the public, it sometimes enters into a formal agreement with an organization to provide those services for a fee. This process is called "purchase of service."

Research Grant: Funds are used to help pay the costs of investigations or experiments (especially those that are academic or scientific in nature).

Scholarship: Money awarded to an individual to further his or her educational training, especially at the undergraduate level. Criteria may be based on scholastic achievement, area of study, financial need, and/or the meeting of certain specific requirements such as "being a resident of XYZ community."

Service Grant: Funds used to underwrite health and other services performed for a particular population group.

Special Revenue Sharing: Federal money given to state and local governments for specific purposes, such as public education. (Compare with *General Revenue Sharing,* page 95.)

Staffing Grant: Money given to an institution to underwrite salaries of professionals, technicians, and in-service training personnel.

Surplus Property: See *Excess and Surplus Property* entry.

Training Grant: Money given to a private or nonprofit organization to support the cost of training personnel. The type of training— and sometimes the type of trainee—is stipulated.

Unsolicited Proposal: A grant or contract proposal sent to the Federal government without the government first formally expressing an official desire to receive such a proposal. An unsolicited proposal might be submitted when, for example, a person comes up with a unique idea.

In addition to the funding mechanisms described above, the Federal government employs many other forms of assistance: guaranteed loans, insurance, counseling, information collection, and dissemination services, to name a few.

APPENDIX J

Glossary

Also see Appendix H, "Types of Grants."

Appropriation: See "Authorization."

Authorization: There is a distinct and vital difference between a congressional "authorization" and "appropriation." When Congress "authorizes" dollars for a federal agency to spend on a program, Congress has approved the budget for a program but has not yet given a federal agency the approval to spend money or to incur obligations on it. The federal agency cannot commit dollars on a program until Congress takes the second step, "appropriating" the dollars. Quite often the amount finally "appropriated" is much smaller than that initially "authorized."

Backdoor Spending: Slang for federal spending that is mandatory on a year-to-year basis, usually because of some existing law. For instance: Social Security and Veteran Benefits. This type of outlay is "relatively uncontrollable" (see "Controllability" definition).

Budget Amendment: When the President wants to change a section of the proposed budget that he has already submitted to Congress, he sends Congress a budget amendment.

Budget Authority: The U.S. Government defines "Budget Authority" as follows: "Authority provided by law to enter into obligations that generally result in outlays. The basic forms of budget authority are appropriations, borrowing authority (statutory authority, not necessarily provided through the appropriations process, that permits federal agencies to incur obligations and make payments from borrowed moneys), and contract authority (statutory authority, not necessarily provided through the appropriations process, that permits federal agencies to enter into contracts or incur other obligations in advance of an appropriation)." *Sic.*

Budget Receipts: The net dollars collected from the public by the Federal government.

Budget Surplus or Deficit: Federal budget receipts minus federal outlays. In the last half century, most years have had deficit balances.

Concurrent Resolution on the Budget: The U.S. Government gives this definition: "A resolution passed by both Houses of Congress, but not requiring the signature of the President, setting forth, reaffirming, or revising specified Congressional budget totals for the Federal Government for a fiscal year."

Continuing Resolution: For a variety of reasons, including procrastination, Congress doesn't get around to authorizing funds for some programs until after the fiscal year begins. If an existing program finds itself in such straits, Congress can vote it interim dollars via a "Continuing Resolution."

Controllability: If funds are controllable, then they may be legally spent or withheld at the will of Congress and the President. If funds are "relatively uncontrollable," their outlay may be dictated by a previously enacted law. Veterans' benefits, for example, are considered to be "relatively uncontrollable."

Deferral: When an Executive Branch member intentionally or unintentionally causes a delay in the availability of appropriated funds, it is referred to as a deferral. Should such a deferral displease Congress, it has the power to force the Executive Branch to spend the funds.

Enabling Legislation: The law that authorizes the grant-making program.

Fiscal Year: The Federal government's official accounting period, running from October 1 through September 30. The year that September 30 falls within determines the numerical designation of a fiscal year.

General Revenue Sharing (GRS): U.S. Treasury funds given to state and local governments to spend (more or less) as they wish. For a more detailed discussion, see the Treasury Department section on page 95.

Grant: See Appendix H, "Types of Grants."

Grantor vs. Grantee: The funding agency is the grantor; the recipient is the grantee.

Impoundment: Occurs when the Executive Branch, by design,

doesn't spend the funds Congress has authorized. Generally, there are two types of impoundments: deferral and rescission (see both).

Local Government: Any governmental unit below the state level. For instance: a county, city, town, or school district.

Obligations: Money that the Federal government promises to pay out for goods or services. Obligations are usually in the form of contracts, purchase orders (for equipment or other material), or salaries (for services rendered).

Outlays: Money that the Federal government has actually spent.

Passed-Through Funds: See "Flow-Through Money."

Prior Approval: Written approval must almost always be obtained from the funding agency if you wish to alter the program or to spend the money in a different way than was originally agreed upon. Failure to receive "prior approval" can result in nonpayment of unapproved expenditures.

Program Director: The individual appointed by the grantee and approved by the grantor to direct a federally funded program. A "program director" may also be referred to as a "project director (PD)" or a "principal investigator (PI)." The latter terminology is favored by The National Science Foundation and certain other research-oriented funding agencies.

Provider: An individual or organization who contractually agrees to provide specified services to or on behalf of the government.

Regulations: Rules that the federal agencies develop to implement laws passed by Congress.

Rescission: Occurs when the President decides to cancel all or part of the funds previously appropriated to a program. If Congress does not approve a rescission within forty-five days, the rescission becomes ineffective.

Slip Law Prints: After the President signs a law, it is published in a pamphlet referred to as a "slip law print." These prints (along with other printed subject matter such as congressional concurrent resolutions and presidential proclamations) are combined into a master *U.S. Statutes at Large* document.

State Government: All fifty states and, with a few exceptions, their agencies. The District of Columbia, the Commonwealth of Puerto Rico, and any territory or possession of the United States are unofficially classified as "state governments."

Stipend: Awarded to students, trainees, et cetera, to defray basic living expenses.

Subnational Government: Any governmental unit (state, county, local, et cetera) below the federal level.

Supplemental Appropriations: Funds Congress makes available to a program or activity other than those originally appropriated for that program or activity. Supplemental appropriations can also include new programs whose needs are so great that they cannot afford to wait until the next regular appropriations period.

U.S. Statutes at Large: see "Slip Law Prints."

Bibliography

Of the hundreds of books we have read pertaining directly or indirectly to government grants, the following are among the ones we believe should be included in a well-stocked, well-rounded government grant-seeker's library:

Academic and Entrepreneurial Research by Ilene N. Bernstein and Howard E. Freeman (Russell Sage Foundation, New York, 1975, 187 pages).

A Citizen's Action Guide: CETA (Center for Community Change, Washington, D.C., 1976, 23 pages).

A Citizen's Action Guide: Economic Development Administration Programs (Center for Community Change, Washington, D.C., 1976, 24 pages).

A Guide to Federal Programs (National Trust for Historic Preservation, Washington, D.C., 1974, 398 pages).

A Guide to Grantsmanship for County Officials (National Association of Counties, Washington, D.C., 1973, 55 pages).

A Guide to Institutional Cost Sharing Agreements (Public Health Service, Washington, D.C., 1974, 11 pages).

A Guide to the NIH Research Contracting Process (National Institutes of Health, Washington, D.C., 1973, 25 pages).

A Manual for Obtaining Government Grants by Louis A. Urgo, Ph.D. (Robert J. Corcoran Company, Boston, 1972, 29 pages).

A-95: What It Is—How It Works (U.S. Government Printing Office, Washington, D.C., 1976, 39 pages).

Annual Register of Grant Support (Marquis Who's Who, Inc., Indianapolis, 1975, 646 pages).

The Art of Fund Raising by Irving R. Warner (Harper & Row, New York, 1975, 176 pages).

The Art of Winning Foundation Grants by Howard Hillman and Karin Abarbanel (Vanguard Press, New York, 1975, 188 pages).

The Budget of the United States Government (U.S. Government Printing Office, Washington, D.C., 1977, 385 pages).

The Businessman's Guide to Washington by William Ruder and Raymond Nathan (Macmillan Publishing Company, New York, 1975, 408 pages).

Capital Ideas by M. Jane Williams (Fund Raising Institute, Plymouth Meeting, Pennsylvania, 1975, three volumes, 1020 pages).

Catalog of Federal Domestic Assistance (U.S. Government Printing Office, Washington, D.C., 1977, 1,046 pages).

Community Based Organizations (U.S. Department of Labor, Washington, D.C., 1974, 81 pages).

The Complete Fund Raising Guide by Howard R. Mirkin (Public Service Materials Center, New York, 1975, 159 pages).

Congressional Directory (U.S. Government Printing Office, Washington D.C., 1976, 1,146 pages).

Congressional Staff Directory by Charles B. Brownson (Congressional Staff Directory, Mount Vernon, Virginia, 1976, 831 pages).

Contracting for Purchase of Services: A Procedural Manual by David S Franklin and Monika White (University of Southern California, Los Angeles, 1975, 69 pages).

Corporate Planning for Nonprofit Organizations by James M. Hardy (Association Press, New York, 1972, 117 pages).

The Costs of Implementing Federally Mandated Social Programs at Colleges and Universities by Carole Van Alstyne and Sharon L. Coldren (American Council on Education, Washington, D.C., 1976, 62 pages).

Cultural Directory (Associated Council for the Arts, New York, 1975, 340 pages).

The D.C. Dialect by Paul Morgan and Sue Scott (Washington Mews Books, New York, 1975, 128 pages).

Directory of Key Government Personnel (Hill and Knowlton, Inc., New York, 1975, 106 pages).

Do or Die: Survival for Nonprofits by James C. Lee (Taft Products, Inc., Washington, D.C., 1974, 102 pages).

Encyclopedia of Governmental Advisory Organizations (Gale Research Company, Detroit, 1975, 668 pages).

Evaluating Action Programs by Carol H. Weiss (Allyn & Bacon, Inc., Boston, 1972, 365 pages).

Federal Funding Guide for Elementary and Secondary Education (Education Funding Research Council, Washington, D.C., 1975, 419 pages).

Federal Funding Guide for Local Governments (Government Information Services, Washington, D.C., 1976, 321 pages).

General Revenue Sharing: The Case for Reform (Center for National Policy Review, Washington, D.C., 1976, 32 pages).

Getting Involved: Your Guide to Revenue Sharing (U.S. Department of the Treasury, Washington, D.C., 1974, 23 pages).

Grants by Virginia P. White (Plenum Press, New York, 1975, 354 pages).

Grants and Aid to Individuals in the Arts (Washington International Arts Letter, Washington, D.C., 1976, 221 pages).

Grants and Awards Available to American Writers (PEN American Center, New York, 1976, 111 pages).

Grants for Scientific Research (National Science Foundation, Washington, D.C., 1973, 43 pages).

Grants From Soup to Nuts by Sally J. Oleon (Queensborough Community College, New York, 1975, 41 pages).

Grantsmanship Is Never Having to Say You're Broke (National Drug Abuse Center, Arlington, Virginia, 1975, 39 pages).

Grants Policy Statement (U.S. Department of Health, Education and Welfare, Washington, D.C., 1974, 74 pages).

Guide to Federal Aid for Cities and Towns by Howard S. Rowland (Quadrangle Books, New York, 1972, 1,312 pages).

Guide to Federal Programs for Rural Development (U.S. Department of Agriculture, Washington, D.C., 1975, 262 pages).

Have Your Way With Bureaucrats by James H. Boren (Chilton Book Company, Radnor, Pa., 1975, 183 pages).

How to Get Government Grants by Philip Des Marais (Public Service Materials Center, New York, 1975, 155 pages).

Human Work for Human Needs (The National Center for Community Change, Washington, D.C., 1975, 225 pages).

The Incentive Grant Approach in Higher Education: A 15-year Record by Martin Finkelstein (George Washington University, Washington, D.C., 1976, 56 pages).

Mediability: A Guide for Nonprofits by Len Biegel and Aileen Lubin (Taft Products, Inc., Washington, D.C., 1975, 110 pages).

Museum Guide to Federal Programs (Association of Science-Technology Centers, Washington, D.C., 1975, 152 pages).

Preparing Instructional Objectives by Robert F. Mager (Fearon Publishers, Inc., Belmont, California, 1975, 136 pages).

R&D Management by John G. Wirt, etc. (D.C. Heath and Company, Lexington, Massachusetts, 1970, 233 pages).

Special Analyses—Budget of the United States Government (U.S. Government Printing Office, Washington, D.C., 1977, 313 pages).

The United States Budget in Brief (U.S. Government Printing Office, Washington, D.C., 1977, 71 pages).

United States Government Manual (General Services Administration, U.S. Government, Washington, D.C., 1976, 871 pages).

Up Your Accountability by Paul Bennett (Taft Products, Inc., Washington, D.C., 1975, 66 pages).

User's Guide to Funding Resources, compiled and edited by Stephen E. Nowlan et al. of Human Resources Network (Chilton Book Company, Radnor, Pa., 1975, 881 pages).

Variations in Research Indirect Cost Rates (Peat, Marwick, Mitchell & Company, New York, 1969, 19 pages).

Where The Money Is (The National Center for Community Action, Washington, D.C., 1975, 106 pages).

INDEX

"A-," circulars prefixed with, 148*n.*,
149–51
AAFRC (American Association of
Fund-Raising Counsel), 155
Abbreviations, 215 ff
Academic Research Information
System (ARIS), 155
ACA Publications, 166
Acknowledgment letter, 52, 53
Acronyms, 215 ff
ACTION, 77–78
Action plan, development of, 8, 58
Addendum to application, 28
Administrative standards, circulars
and, 148 ff
Administrators, grant, 12
ADPE (automatic data-processing
equipment), 153
Aerospace projects, 89–90
Aged, programs for, 73
Agencies, personnel of. *See* Offi-
cers, funding program.
Agency for International Develop-
ment (AID), 92–93
Agriculture, Department of, 78
retrieval system of, 169
Aid to Families with Dependent
Children (AFDC), 72, 88–
89
Alabama information centers, 140,
174
Alcohol, Drug Abuse, and Mental
Health Administration
(ADAMHA), 67
Almanac of congressional events,
164
American Association of Fund-
Raising Counsel (AAFRC),
155
American Education, 66, 190
A-95 Clearinghouse Review Sys-
tem, 150, 203 ff

Annual Register of Grant Support,
156
Annual reports, 28
Appalachian Regional Commission
(ARC), 78
Application, grant, 22 ff
preparation of, 22 ff
addendum and, 28
best person for, 41–42
budget conception and, 30 ff
deadlines and, 43
description of project and,
26–28
designee of money and, 29
documentation and, 28–29
errors common in, 22 ff
feedback and, 30
information sources for, 42
instructions for, 23, 48
legal blind spots and, 29
procrastination in, 23–24
writing tips for, 24–26
wrong form/instructions for,
22–23
review of, 46 ff
deferred decision and, 54
failure and, reasons for, 50,
53–54
negotiation and, 51
questions evaluators ask, 48–
50
submission of, 43–45
Apprenticeship programs, 211
Appropriation, 226
Aris Funding Messenger, 155
Arizona information centers, 140
Arkansas information center, 141
Arts programs, 101–3, 188
Assistance Payments Administration, 72
Assistant secretaries, form of address for, 213

Associated Councils of the Arts, 166
Association of Science-Technology Centers, 181
Auditing by government, 55–56
Authorization, 130, 226
Automatic data-processing equipment (ADPE), 153

Backdoor spending, 226
Basic Educational Opportunity Grants (BEOG), 66, 208–9
Beneficiaries of project, 26–27
Bibliographies, GPO individual subject, 175
Bidding, *Commerce Business Daily* and, 162
Bills, congressional
    copies of, 165
    pending, 156–57, 198–200
Block grants, definition of, 222
Bookstores, GPO, 174–75
Brakeley, John Price Jones, 157
Budget, federal
    amendment, 226
    authority, 226
    concurrent resolution on, 227
    publications of, 157–59
    receipts, 227
    surplus or deficit, 227
    Zero-Based, 196
Budget of project, 30 ff
    changes in, after approval, 55
    cost-sharing and, 39–40
    directs costs, 32–33, 34 ff
    equipment and, 36
    final report on, 56
    indirect costs, 33, 40
    matching funds and, 40–41
    miscellaneous category in, 37
    negotiation of, 51
    outside services and, 35
    personnel and, 34–35
    rent and, 35
    sample of, 38–39
    size of, 31
    supplies and, 36
    time factor and, 32
    touchy items in, 32
    travel and meetings and, 36–37
    utilities and, 35–36

Budget and Impoundment Control Act (1974), 200
Budget Information System (BIS), 145
Budget of U.S. Government, 157–59
Bureaucracy, 201–2
Bureau of Educational and Cultural Affairs, 92
Businessman's Guide to Washington, 159
Business programs, 91

Cabinet members, forms of address for, 212
California information centers, 141, 174
Capital Ideas, 172
Capitation grant, 222
Caribbean programs, 85
Catalog, GPO Monthly, 175–76
Catalog of Federal Domestic Assistance, 12, 112, 124 ff, 137, 158
    appendixes, 131–32
    indexes, 124 ff
        agency program, 125
        applicant eligibility, 125–26
        popular name, 126
        subject, 126–27
    limitations of, 133–34
    ordering of, 132–33
    program changes section, 127
    program descriptions section, 127 ff
    supplement, 132
Categorical grant, 222
CBD (*Commerce Business Daily*), 161–62
Center for Community Change, 159
Center for Disease Control (CDC), 67–68
Centers, Federal Information, 140 ff
CEP (Cooperative Education Program), 210
CFR (*Code of Federal Regulations*), 137, 161
Check list of questions
    evaluators ask, 48–50
    for funding officials, 15–16

Chilton Book Company, 179
Chronicle of Higher Education, 190
Circulars, federal, 148 ff
Cities, information on, 84–85, 160
Clearinghouse, Funding Sources, 171–72
Clearinghouse Review System (A-95), 150, 203 ff
Code of Federal Regulations (CFR), 137, 161
Collective approach, 59
College Resource Development Service, 190
"College and University Reporter," 190
College Work Study Program, 210
Colorado information centers, 141, 174
Commerce, Department of, 79
Commerce Business Daily, 161–62
Commissioners, form of address for, 213
Committees, congressional
    proposed legislation and, 199
    publications of, 165
    stating your case to, 58
Community Action Program, 80
Community Based Organizations, 89
Community Development Block Grant Assistance Program, 84
Community Development Corporations, 80
Community leaders, 20
Community Services Administration (CSA), 80
Competition for grants, 7, 21
Comprehensive Employment and Training Act (CETA), 88, 89
Concurrent resolution on budget, 227
Conference grant, definition of, 222
Congressional bills
    copies of, 165
    proposed, 156–57, 198–200
Congressional Boxscore, 167, 173
Congressional committees. *See* Committees, congressional.

Congressional Directory, 165
Congressional Quarterly Weekly Report, 163–64
Congressional Record, 164
Congressional Research Service, 180
Congressional Staff Directory, 164–65
Congressmen, 19–20
    forms of address for, 214
    influence of, 19–20
    information from, 20
Connecticut information centers, 141
Consortium grant, definition of, 222
Construction grant, definition of, 222
Consultation fees, 35
Contacts, cultivation of, 11 ff
Continuing education grant, definition of, 222
Continuing research grant, definition of, 222–23
Continuing resolution, definition of, 227
Contract, grant vs., 224
Contracting for Purchase of Services, 165
Contract-seekers, information for, 161–62, 165, 169–70
Contributions to project, 35, 40
Controllability, 227
Cooperative Education Program, 210
Coordinator, grant, 41–42
Copies of congressional bills, 165
Corporate grant, definition of, 223
Correspondence with officials, 18
    forms of address for, 212–14
Costs, project, 30 ff. *See also* Budget of project.
    direct, 32–33, 34 ff
    indirect, 33, 40
Cost-sharing, 39–40, 224
County News, 181
Creative Annual Reports, 28–29
Credibility factor, 58
Crime programs, 86–87
CUED Commentary, 160
Cultural Directory, 165–66
Cultural Post, 103

Cultural programs, 91–92, 100 ff, 165–66, 188

Deadlines
  application, 43
  for postproject report, 57
Decision-making
  aftermath of, 52 ff
  application review and, 46 ff
  officials and, 13
Defense, Department of, 80–81
Deferral of application, 54
Deferral of funds, 200, 227
Delivery of application, 44
Demonstration grant, definition of, 223
Departmental hierarchy, 17
Departments. *See* area of authority, *e.g.,* Justice, Department of.
Depository Libraries, 166
Deputy secretaries, form of address for, 213
Description of programs (in *Catalog*), 127 ff
Description of your project, 26–28
Designee of funds, 29
Dial-a-Reg, 139
Directory of Key Government Personnel, 167
Directory of Research Grants, 184
Discretionary grant, definition of, 223
District of Columbia. *See* Washington, D.C.
Documentation for application, 28–29
Documents Room, 165
Donated services, 35, 40
Drug abuse agency, 67
Drug Abuse Materials Distribution Center, 178

Economic Development Assistance (EDA), 79
Economic Development Program (of CSA), 80
Educational Opportunity Grants, 208, 209
Educational programs, 65–67, 208 ff, 222
  information sources for, 167–68, 190

Educational Researcher, 190
Educational Resources Newsletter, 190
Education Division of HEW, 65–67
Education Funding News, 167
Education Funding Research Council (EFRC), 167–68
EEOC (Equal Opportunity Commission), 82
Eligibility index in *Catalog,* 125–26
Employment and Training Administration (ETA), 87–89
Enabling legislation, 227
Encyclopedia of Associations, 168
Encyclopedia of Governmental Advisory Organizations, 168–69
Energy Research and Development Administration (ERDA), 81
Entertainment of officials, 16
Entitlement grant, definition of, 223
Environmental Protection Agency (EPA), 81–82
Equal Employment Opportunity Commission (EEOC), 82
Equipment costs, 36
Evaluators, application, 48–50
Excess-property programs, 83–84, 223
Expenses, project, 30 ff. *See also* Budget of project.

Faculty Alert Bulletin, 184
Failure of proposal, 50–51, 53–54
Federal Aid to States, 113
Federal Assistance Programs: How to Get . . . , 180
Federal Assistance Programs Retrieval System (FAPRS), 169
Federal Aviation Administration (FAA), 94
Federal Contracts Report, 169
Federal Council of the Arts and Humanities, 100
Federal Depository Libraries, 166
Federal Energy Administration (FEA), 82–83
Federal Executive Boards (FEBs), 147

Federal Funding Guide for Elementary and Secondary Education, 167

Federal Funding Guide for Local Governments, 173

Federal Highway Administration, 94

Federal Information Centers, 140 ff

Federal Management Circulars (FMCs), 148, 151 ff

Federal Notes, 170

Federal Outlays, 185

Federal Regional Councils (FRCs), 145–47

Federal Register, 135 ff, 200
  language in, example of, 136
  ordering of, 138–39
  sections of, 137–38

Federal Register Report, 173

Federal Research Report, 171

Feedback on application, 30

Fellowship, definition of, 223

Financial Assistance by Geographic Area (HEW), 73–74

FIPSE (Fund for the Improvement of Postsecondary Education), 65

Fiscal year, 227

Florida information centers, 141, 174

Flow-through money, 223–24

FMCs (Federal Management Circulars), 148, 151 ff

Food and Drug Administration, 68

Form 424, 186

Forms, grant-application, 22. *See also* Application, grant.

Formula grant, definition of, 224

Foundation grants
  definition of, 224
  differences of, from government grants, 3

FRC (Federal Regional Council) system, 145–47, 170

Freedom of Information Act, 118

FRI (Fund Raising Institute), 172

Fringe benefits, budget preparation and, 33–34

FSC (Funding Sources Clearinghouse), 171–72

Fund Development & Technical Assistance Report, 180

Fund for the Improvement of Postsecondary Education, 65

Funding program officers, 12 ff. *See also* Officers, funding program.

Funding Sources Clearinghouse, 171–72

Fund Raising Institute (FRI), 172

Fund Raising Management, 170–71

Funds
  designee of, 29
  surplus, 57

Fund Sources in Health and Allied Fields, 184

Future of government grants, 196

Gale Research Company, 168, 169

General Revenue Sharing (GRS), 95–96, 227

General Services Administration (GSA), 83–84, 148n., 223

Genesis of grants, 198–200

Geographic & Executive Index, 168

Georgetown University Workshop, 172

Georgia information centers, 141, 174

G.I. Bill, 210–11

Gifts-in-kind, 40, 224

Glossary, 226 ff

Goals of project
  defining of, 6, 8
  description of, 27
  negotiation of, 51

Government grant, definition of, 224

Government Information Services (GIS), 172

Government Printing Office, 119–20
  bibliographies on selected subjects, 175
  bookstores, 174–75
  Monthly Catalog, 175–76
  Selected U.S. Government Publications, 176

Government R&D Report, 173

GPO. *See* Government Printing Office.

Grant Development Institute, 176

Grant Information System, 184

Grantor vs. grantee, 227
Grants
administrators of, 12
bureaucracy and, 201–2
contracts vs., 224
coordinators of, 41–42
genesis of, 198–200
history and trends of, 195–97
-in-aid, definition of, 224
phases of seeking, 3 ff. *See also*
Phases of grant-seeking.
types of, 222 ff
Grants Administration (National
Graduate University), 183
Grants Administration Manual
(HEW), 73
Grants Administration Policies
(SRS), 72
*Grants and Aid to Individuals in
the Arts,* 188
*Grants and Awards Available to
American Writers,* 177
*Grants: How to Find Out About
Them* . . . , 176–77
Grantsmanship Center, 177–78
*Grantsmanship Is Never Having to
Say You're Broke,* 178
Grants Policy Statement (PHS),
71
Grants Register, 178
Grants for Scientific Research, 108
GRS (General Revenue Sharing),
95–96, 227
GSA (General Services Adminis-
tration), 83–84, 148n., 223
Guide to Federal Programs, 178–
79
*Guide to Financial Aid for Stu-
dents and Parents,* 211
*Guide to Institutional Cost Sharing
Agreements* . . . , 40
*Guidelines for Submitting Pro-
posals* (HUD), 85
Guide to Programs (NEA), 102,
103
Guide to Programs (NSF), 108

Handbook, official, of U.S. govern-
ment, 187
Hawaii information center, 141
Health, Education, and Welfare
(HEW), Department of,
63 ff

Education Division, 65–67
information on, where to writ
for, 74–76
Office of Human Development
71–72
publications, 66, 69, 70–71, 73·
74
Public Health Service, 67 ff
regional addresses, 74–75
Social and Rehabilitation Serv·
ice, 72
Social Security Administration
72–73
Health Resources Administration
(HRA), 68–69
Health Resources News, 69
Health Services Administration
(HSA), 69
Hierarchy of agency personnel, 1ⁱ
*Higher Education and Nationa
Affairs,* 190
Hill and Knowlton, Inc., 167
History of government financia·
assistance, 195
House of Representatives. *See als*
Congressmen; Congres-
sional *entries.*
proposed bills and, 198–99
Housing and Urban Development
(HUD), Department of
84–85
How to Do Business with DHEW
74
How to Get Money for . .
(series), 179
HUD Newsletter and *Challenge*
85
Humanistic study, 104–6
Humanities (newsletter), 106
Human Resources Network, 179
Human Work for Human Needs
182

ICMA Newsletter, 160
Illinois information centers, 141,
174
Impoundment, 227–28
Impoundment Control Act (1974),
200
*Incentive Grant Approach in
Higher Education,* 190
Independent agencies, 97–98, 100 ff

ndiana information center, 141
nfluence, political, 19, 111–12
nformation sources, 117 ff
  for application preparation, 42
  Catalog of Federal Domestic Assistance, 12, 112, 124 ff, 137, 158
  circulars, 148 ff
  congressmen as, 20
  for contract-seekers, 161–62, 165, 169–70
  Federal Information Centers, 140 ff
  Federal Register, 135 ff, 200
  form letter for, 121
  Freedom of Information Act and, 118
  general tip on, 118 ff
  Government Printing Office, 119–20
  inaccessible, 11
  insufficient, 10
  for local government programs, 112
  long-term thinking and, 68
  meetings with officials and, 13 ff
  noncentralized, 10
  obstacles to, 9–10
  outdated, 10
  private organizations as, 122–23, 155 ff
  regional councils, 145–47
  researching of opportunities, 9–11
  sharing of, 21
  specialized, 189–91
  for state programs, 112
  for student aid, 211
Institute for Fund-Raising, 179
Institute of Medicine, 109
Instructions for grant application, 23, 48
Inter-American Foundation, 85
Interchange, 89
Intergovernmental Relations and Regional Operations Division, 206
Interior, Department of, 86
International City Management Association, 160
Iowa information center, 141

Jargon, 25
Job Corps, 88
Justice, Department of, 86

Kansas information centers, 141
Kentucky information center, 141
Key officials, directory of, 167

Labor, Department of, 87–89
Latin American programs, 85
Law Enforcement Assistance Administration (LEAA), 86
Lawson Associates, 180
Leaders in field of interest, 21
Legal blind spots, 29
Legislation, 130
  copies of, 165
  enabling, 227
  historical, 195
  pending, 156–57, 198–200
Legislative Bulletin, 160
"Legislative Status Report," 167
Leisure Information Service, 180
Lexington Books, 185
Libraries, Depository, 166
Library of Congress, 180
Library of information, building your own, 10–11
Loans, student, 209–10
Local government
  agencies, 95–96, 110 ff
  definition of, 228
  information on programs of, 112
  Regional Councils and, 145–47
Local Government Funding Report, 173
Long-term thinking, 58–59
Louisiana information center, 141
LRC-W Newsbriefs, 180–81
Lutheran Council in America, 180–81

Macmillan Publishing Company, 159
Mailing of application, 44
Maritime Administration, 79
Marquis Who's Who, 156
Marts & Lundy, 181
Maryland information center, 141
Massachusetts information centers, 141, 174
Masterman, Louis E., 50

Matching funds, 40–41, 224
  arts endowments and, 102
Medical Services Administration,
  72
Meetings
  expenses of, 36–37
  with officials, 13 ff
  stating your case at, 58
Methods in project, 27
Michigan information centers, 141,
  174
Minnesota information center, 141
Missouri information centers, 141,
  174
Monthly Catalog (GPO), 175–76
Mosaic, 109
Municipal Year Book, 160
*Museum Guide to Federal Pro-
  grams,* 181

Names of officials, obtaining, 12,
  18
National Academy of Engineering,
  109
National Academy of Sciences, 109
National Aeronautics and Space
  Administration (NASA),
  89–90
National Association of Counties
  (NACo), 181–82
National Center for Community
  Action (NCCA), 182
National Center for Education
  Statistics, 65
National Council on the Arts, 103
National Council on the Humani-
  ties, 105
National Council on Philanthropy
  (NCOP), 182
National Council of University
  Research Administrators,
  190
National Council for Urban Eco-
  nomic Development, 160
National Direct Student Loan, 209
National Drug Abuse Materials
  Distribution Center, 178
National Endowment for the Arts
  (NEA), 40–41, 101–3
National Endowment for the Hu-
  manities (NEH), 104–6
National Foundation on the Arts
  and Humanities, 100 ff

National Graduate University,
  182–83
National Institute of Education
  (NIE), 65
National Institutes of Health
  (NIH), 69–71
  Guide for Grants and Contracts,
  71
National Journal, 183
National League of Cities, 160
National Oceanic and Atmospheric
  Administration, 79
National Organizations of the U.S.,
  168
National Research Council, 109
National Science Board, 107
National Science Foundation
  (NSF), 106 ff
National Technical Information
  Service, 133, 185
National Trust for Historic Preser-
  vation, 179
Nation's Cities, 160
Nebraska information center, 141
Need for project, 26
Negotiation, postsubmission, 51
New Associations & Projects, 168
New County Times, 181
New Federalism, 196
New Jersey information centers,
  141
New Mexico information centers,
  141
Newspapers, 183
New York information centers,
  141, 174
New York Times, 183
New York University Seminars,
  183–84
NLC Washington Report, 160
North Carolina information cen-
  ter, 141
Notices section in *Register,* 138
Notification of funding decision,
  52
Notification of Intent (NOI), 205
Nuclear Regulatory Commission
  (NRC), 90
Number, program, 129

Objectives of project
  defining, 6, 8
  description of, 27

bligations, 228
)ffice of Comprehensive Employ-
    ment Development
    (OCED), 88–89
)ffice of Education (OE), 65–66,
    209
  operating units of, 66
)ffice of Human Development
    (OHD), 71–72
)ffice of Management and Budget
    (OMB), 113, 133–34, 206
  circulars and, 148*n.*, 154
)fficers, funding program, 12 ff
  congressmen and, 19
  deadline date acquisition from,
    43–44
  decision-making power of, 13
  directory of, 167
  entertainment of, 16
  hierarchy of, 17
  keeping in touch with, 59
  meeting with, 13 ff
  names of, obtaining, 12, 18
  on-site visits by, 16, 56
  questions for, 14–16
  regional, 17
  review process and, 47
  thank-you letter to, 53
)gilvy, David, 6
)hio information centers, 141,
    174
)klahoma information centers,
    141
)MB. *See* Office of Management
    and Budget.
)n-site visits by officials, 16, 56
)pinions, expression of your, 58–
    59
)pportunities, researching of, 9 ff
)regon information center, 141
)ryx Press, 184
)utlays, 228
)utside services, budgeting for, 35
)verseas Relief Grants, 93

'aperwork, federal, 201
'ayments, state and local agency,
    111
'eer review, 46–47
'.E.N. American Center, 177
'ennsylvania information centers,
    141, 174
'eople-to-people programs, 92

Personnel
  agency. *See* Officers, funding
    program.
  directory of, 167
  project, budgeting for, 34–35
Phases of grant-seeking, 3 ff
  one: preliminaries, 5 ff
  two: researching, 9 ff
  three: preparing application,
    22 ff
  four: submitting application,
    43 ff
  five: review of application, 46 ff
  six: after decision is made, 52 ff
Plan of action, development of, 8,
    58
Planning grant, 224
Plenum Press, 177
PNRS (Project Notification and
    Review System), 204–6
Political influence, 19
  state and locally administered
    programs and, 111–12
Popular name index in *Catalog,*
    126
Poverty programs, 77, 78, 80
Preliminaries of grant-seeking, 5 ff
  defining goal, 6
  determining whether grant is for
    you, 7–8
  plan of action, 8
  reversing the roles, 5–6
  sales proposition, 6–7
President of Senate, form of ad-
    dress for, 213
President of U.S.
  form of address for, 212
  grant genesis and, 198, 200–201
Presidential Documents, 189
Principal investigator (PI), 228
Prior approval, 228
Private organizations, information
    from, 122–23, 155 ff
Procrastination in preparing appli-
    cation, 23–24
Profiles of Grant Programs, 71
Program Announcements (NEH),
    106
Program director (PD), 228
Project
  budget, 30 ff
  conducting of, 54–56
  description, 26–28

Project (*cont.*)
  grant, definition of, 224
  proposals. *See* Application,
    grant.
  termination of, 56–57
Project Notification and Review
    System, 204–6
Promotion of Industry and Com-
    merce, 79
Proposals. *See* Application, grant.
Proposed legislation, 156–57, 198–
    200
Proposed rules and regulations, 138
Proposition, unique selling, 6–7
Protocol, forms of address in, 212–
    14
Provider, 228
Public Health Service, 67 ff
  agencies of, 67
  publications of, 70–71
Public Management, 160
Public relations programs, 96
Public Service Materials Center
    (PSMC), 184–85
Publishing of final report, 57
Purchase of service (POS), 224–25

Quasi-governmental agencies,
    100 ff
Questions
  by evaluators, 28, 48–50
  for officials, 14–16

R&D Management, 185
Reception agencies, state, 186
Records, 10–11. *See also* Informa-
    tion sources.
  audits and, 55–56
Regional Action Planning Com-
    missions (RAPC), 79
Regional Councils, 145–47
Regional offices, 17
*Register, Annual, of Grant Sup-
    port,* 156
Register, Federal, 135 ff, 200
Regulations
  definition of, 228
  new and revised, 137–38
  published code of, 137, 161
Rejection of proposal, 50–51, 53–
    54
Rent, budgeting for, 35
Reports

  annual, 28
  final, 56–57
  publishing of, 57
Representatives, U.S. *See* Con-
    gressmen.
Requests for Proposals (RFPs),
    162
Rescission of funds, 200, 228
Research grants, definition of, 225
Researching your opportunities,
    9 ff
  community leaders and, 20
  competition and, 21
  congressmen and, 19–20
  contacts and, 11 ff
  field of interest and, leaders in,
    21
  information-gathering and, 9–11
  officers of programs and, 12 ff
Resolutions, congressional, 227
Results, reporting on project, 56–
    57
Retrieval services, 167, 169, 173
Revenue sharing, 95–96, 227
Reversing the roles, 5–6
Review of application, 46 ff
Review system (A-95), 203 ff
Rhode Island information center,
    141
Role reversal, 5–6
Roosevelt, Franklin D., 195
Rules, new and revised, 137–38
Rural Development Service, 169

St. Martin's Press, 178
Salaries, project, 34–35
Sales proposition for project, 6–7
SBA (Small Business Administra-
    tion), 91
SCENYU, 183–84
Scholarship, definition of, 225
Science and Technology (Depart-
    ment of Commerce), 79
Scientific projects, 79, 106 ff
SCIRA (State Central Informa-
    tion Reception Agencies),
    186
*Selected Information Sources for
    Urban Specialists,* 85
*Selected U.S. Government Pub-
    lications,* 176
Selective Depository Library, 166

Seminars
  Institute for Fund-Raising, 179
  National Graduate University,
    182–83
  New York University, 183–84
Senate, proposed bills and, 199
Senators, forms of address for, 214
Service grant, definition of, 225
Services
  information, 122–23, 155 ff
  outside, budgeting for, 35
"Signing off" procedure, 205
Slip law prints, 228
Small Business Administration
    (SBA), 91
Smithsonian Institution, 91–92
  Science Information Exchange
    (SSIE), 186
  Traveling Exhibition Service,
    128–29
Social and Rehabilitation Service
    (SRS), 72
Social-science studies, 104
Social Security Administration
    (SSA), 72–73
Soft contributions, 40
Soup to Nuts, 185–86
Space projects, 89–90
Speaker of the House, form of
    address for, 214
Special Analysis O, 113
SSCE, 172
Staffing grant, definition of, 225
Staff members, agency. See also
    Officers, funding program.
  regional, 17
Standards, administrative, circulars
    and, 148 ff
State, Department of, 92–93
State Central Information Recep-
    tion Agencies, 186
State government
  agencies, 95–96, 110 ff
  clearinghouses, 204, 205
  Regional Councils and, 145–47
  student aid and, 211
Statutes at Large, U.S., 228
Stipend, 229
Student aid, 208 ff
  apprenticeship programs, 211
  BEOG program, 208–9
  cooperative education program,
    210

G.I. Bill, 210–11
  information sources, 211
  loans, 209
  state programs, 211
  supplemental grants, 209
  work study program, 210
Subject index in Catalog, 126–27
Subnational government, 229
Successful Grantsmanship Kit, 176
Sunset system, 196
Superintendent of Documents, 120
Supplemental appropriations, defi-
    nition of, 229
Supplemental Educational Oppor-
    tunity Grants, 209
Supplies, costs of, 36
Surplus funds, 57
Surplus-property programs, 83–84,
    223

Taft Corporation, 187
Tamblyn & Brown, 187
Target of project, 26–27
TC-1082, 150, 186
Technical Information Service,
    133, 185
Telephone numbers
  for bill-status information, 156
  Federal Information Center,
    140 ff
  Register information, 139
  Washington, D.C., directory of,
    166–67
Tennessee information centers, 141
Tennessee Valley Authority
    (TVA), 93–94
Termination of project, 56–57
Texas information centers, 143,
    174
Thank-you letter, 52, 53
Time factors
  deadline for application, 43
  length of project, 32
  postproject reports and, 57
  review of proposal, 46–47
Title XX program, 72
Training grant, definition of, 225
Transportation, Department of,
    94–95
Travel expenses, 36–37
Treasury, Department of, 95–96,
    113
Treasury Circular 1082, 150, 186,

Trends in government financial assistance, 196–97
TVA (Tennessee Valley Authority), 93–94
Types of grants, 222 ff

Undersecretaries, forms of address for, 213
Unemployment Insurance Service (UIS), 89
Unique selling proposition, 6–7
United States Employment Service (USES), 89
United States Government Manual, 187
United States Information Agency (USIA), 96–97
Unsolicited proposal, 225
Urban Corps, 210
Urban Mass Transportation Administration, 94
Urban programs, 84–85, 160
Utah information centers, 143
Utilities, budgeting for, 35–36

Veterans Administration, 97
  G.I. Bill and, 210–11
Vice President, form of address for, 212

"VIP Proposal Delivery," 167, 17
Visits, on-site, by officials, 16, 56
Volunteered services, 35, 40

Washington, D.C.
  information centers, 141, 174
  telephone directory, 166–67
"Washington Hotline," 167, 173
Washington Information Director
  188
Washington International Arts Le
  ter, 188
Washington Post, 183
Washington (state) information
  centers, 143, 174
Weekly Compilation of Presiden
  tial Documents, 189
Where the Money Is, 182
Wisconsin information centers,
  143, 174
Work Incentive Program (WIN)
  88
Workshops, Grantsmanship Cen
  ter, 177
Work Study Program, 210
Writers, 177
Writing style, tips on, 24–26

Zero-Based Budgeting, 196